THE SEVEN CHURCHES OF ASIA

REVELATION 2-3

by

SAMUEL R. SIDERS

authorHOUSE®

AuthorHouse™
1663 Liberty Drive, Suite 200
Bloomington, IN 47403
www.authorhouse.com
Phone: 1-800-839-8640

First published by AuthorHouse 11/20/2007

ISBN: 978-1-4343-4789-3 (sc)
ISBN: 978-1-4343-4788-6 (hc)

Library of Congress Control Number: 2007908379

Printed in the United States of America
Bloomington, Indiana

This book is printed on acid-free paper.

~ Contents ~

~ PREFACE ~

In the fall of 2005 the Lord told me to write about the Seven Churches of Asia written in Revelation chapters 2 and 3. When it became possible for me to begin the research to interpret these chapters as accurately as I possibly could, I also prayed that the Lord would help me to know what to write and not to leave anything out nor add to it anymore than He intended. The end result continues to astonish me to this day.

During the year it took me to write it, I cried, I laughed, and I got convicted. The content is no more than what He has had me to share with others since 1982, primarily that without obedience to God Revival will not come. This book has much more expanded on this subject than anything He has had me to write or say before He gave me this responsibility. It is obvious to me that what He said to these seven churches is a controversial subject, but the Bible gives evidence that what is written herein is a fact.

God requires far more of us than what most Believers are willing to live out, in their walk with God, and in refusing to comply could mean being rejected at the Judgment seat of Christ, where all Believers will stand to be Judged. **You will need to read the entire book to understand what is meant by the previous sentence.** Having shared the manuscript of this book with a number of other Believers in Christ, it has had a positive and sobering effect on those who have read it. This book contains a message all Believers need to hear; that is why it has been published.

For me, this book has been a gift from God to write, primarily because of the fellowship I had with Him all of 2006, to show me what to write, and to help me to understand scriptures I had questioned for years.

It is my sincere prayer for those who will read this book, that God will make its content a positive life changing event that will cause them to know Him in the fullness of His character and personality, what it is to fellowship and walk with God, and to do it moment by moment.

Your brother and fellow servant in Christ,

SAMUEL R. SIDERS

CHAPTER 1
~ EXPLANATIONS AND CAUSES ~

The purpose of this book is not to be another exhortation to live holy, **but rather to obey God.** <u>Holiness, piety, righteous living is the manifested fruit of obedience to God.</u> The righteous nature of God that is planted in our spirit, when we repent of our sin, out of a heart of sincerity and truth (giving us the born-again experience), compels us to obey God. While it is the sinful nature that is still bound in our flesh that constantly wars against our performing what is our new nature to do, <u>which is to obey God's perfect will for our life instead of sin.</u>

> **For I delight in the law of God after the inward man: But I see another law in my members, warring against the law of my mind (*spirit*), and bringing me into captivity to the law of sin which is in my members.**
> **Romans 7:22-23**

The Holy Spirit is the One who removes the sinful nature that is in our spirit and replaces it with the righteous nature of God. As a result of this change God no longer is just our Creator, He now becomes our Father (scripture refers to this as adoption), and we take on the role of a son and daughter. In God's sight we are no longer Sinners, but now we are Saints.

**For ye have not received the spirit of bondage again to fear;
but ye have received the Spirit of adoption, whereby we cry,
Abba, Father.**

Romans 8:15

**To redeem them that were under the law, that we might
receive the adoption of sons.**

Galatians 4:5

God's status for the Sinner is Creator, but His status for the Saint is Creator and Father. The Sinner is under the wrath of God, while the Saint is under the favor of God. God being able to get through to us the revelation that we are a Sinner in need of a Savior, and the knowledge that there is a fiery judgment awaiting us if we do not repent, compelled us to give our heart to Him. Knowing the judgment of God toward the Sinner causes us to compel others as God compelled us, to REPENT.

**Knowing therefore the terror of the Lord, we persuade men;
but we are made manifest unto God; and I trust also are made
manifest in your consciences.**

2 Corinthians 5:11

This book is not intended to be an exhaustive commentary on Revelation chapters two and three. God has a standard of holiness that can only be fulfilled in and through our flesh, when we obey His perfect will. We cannot obey God's perfect will for our life without the power of the Holy Spirit; this power is given to us when we ask God for this greater anointing, found in receiving the baptism of the Holy Spirit, with whom the Power and the Gifts are associated.

**But ye shall receive power, after that the Holy Ghost is come
upon you: and ye shall be witnesses unto me...**

Acts 1:8a

**And they were all filled with the Holy Ghost, and began to
speak with other tongues, as the Spirit gave them utterance.**

Acts 2:4

The book of Acts clearly shows that the work of salvation (being born-again), and the receiving of God's Power are two separate experiences given by the Holy Spirit.

> **Who, when they were come down, prayed for them, that they might receive the Holy Ghost: (For as yet he was fallen upon none of them: only they were baptized in the name of the Lord Jesus.)**
>
> **Acts 8:15-16**

> **When they heard this, they were baptized in the name of the Lord Jesus. And when Paul had laid his hands upon them, the Holy Ghost came on them; and they spake with tongues, and prophesied.**
>
> **Acts 19:5-6**

It is without this "Power" that causes many, who do not have it, to create their own "moral code" to justify their disobedience and inability on their own to obey God's perfect will as Jesus obeyed, deceiving themselves in believing that God is satisfied with their meager effort to comply with His will. Anything less than obeying God's "perfect will" is unacceptable behavior toward God; which not only will engage His wrath against us, and dependant on the severity of our willful and defiant disobedience (rebellion) could jeopardize the salvation of our soul when we pass from this life. I write, "could" because God is the Eternal Judge of all such matters.

> **Be watchful, and strengthen the things which remain, that are ready to die: for I have not found thy works perfect before God.**
>
> **Revelation 3:2**

You will see the facts of these previous paragraphs unfold in what God says to these seven churches, and **what He is saying to us as individual's,** whether we fall under the category of "Religious", "Hypocrite", "Lukewarm", or a true "Saint of God." Christian means "Christ-like" or "loyal and committed to Christ", meaning that Jesus is our Example and Commander of what is acceptable behavior for us to receive the **favor of God instead of God's wrath.**

> **For even hereunto were ye called: because Christ also suffered for us, leaving us an example, that ye should follow his steps:**
> **1 Peter 2:21**

> **If ye love me, keep my commandments.**
> **John 14:15**

Sometime during the near nineteen years before I gave my heart to the Lord, it had gotten into my spirit that God's people are perfect. The understanding I had was that they did not sin. The problem was, I never saw any who fit that description. It wasn't until after I gave my heart to Him, and having Him teach me about this truth, that I received a more correct understanding of what perfection in the sight of God is, and finding "Christians" who don't know anymore than I did, before I got saved. Most Christians believe the "world's" definition of perfection, thus unable to believe that we can be.

God's definition of perfection is not the "world's" definition. **All perfection is, in the sight of God, is obeying Him,** something Jesus did all of the days of His life. It is with Him doing it, that He has left us the instructions to do it, and access to the Teacher who can teach and help us to do so.

> **For even hereunto were ye called: because Christ also suffered for us, leaving us an example, that ye should follow his steps: Who did no sin.... That we, being dead to sins, should live unto righteousness:**
> **1 Peter 2:21-24**

> **But the Comforter, which is the Holy Ghost, whom the Father will send in my name, he shall teach you all things, and bring all things to your remembrance.**
> **John 14:26**

The instructions to obey God is in the written word, the instructions how to obey the written word is given to us by the Holy Spirit. Walking with the Holy Spirit varies with each of us, for we are not all on the same level, and there are many variables that determine how well we learn, and how long it takes to learn whatever the Holy Spirit is wanting to teach us. The sooner we die to self-will, self-ambition, and self-desire, the faster we learn how to accomplish God's definition of perfection, which is total obedience to His desire for us, His perfect will. Anything less will not please or satisfy Him.

1973 is when the Lord gave me my first profound revelation of the ability that He has put within us, who have the endowment of power spoken of in Acts 1:8. Power not only to be effective verbal witnesses for Him, but also the ability to live what we preach being <u>living</u> testimonies. The Greek word for power here means, "Mighty Power."

But ye shall receive *(mighty)* **power, after that the Holy Ghost is come upon you:**

Acts 1:8a

May 8, 1975 the Lord gave me a song titled "A Living Sacrifice", here are the words:

Jesus gave His life for you and me
That from sin and bondage we could be free
Jesus gave Himself a living sacrifice
And for this reason Jesus gave His life
Chorus
There came a day I had to repent
And give my life to Jesus to live for Him
He spilt His blood so I could be cleansed
And from this time on I will live for Him
Chorus
I am weak but Jesus is strong
And by His grace through faith to Him I belong
I will give my life to Jesus a sacrifice
To dwell in His rest and have eternal life
Chorus
Listen my friend here what Jesus says to you
Just as he loves me, He loves you too
Give Jesus your life a living sacrifice
We must die to sin to have eternal life

CHORUS

Thank you Jesus for saving my soul
Thank you Jesus for making me whole
My life I give to you a living sacrifice
Jesus the anointed, the Son, the Holy Christ

In 1981 I was given a book to read, authored by Loran Helm (A Voice In The Wilderness), an autobiography with the primary focus on the work God had done in him to bring him to a place of total obedience to God's expectations for him. When God said it, he did it. With God's help he was faithful to obey to the day of his departure from this life. Preaching the message of obedience to God, and his prayer for revival.

In 1982 the Lord took me into a place of fellowship with Him that very few Christians throughout the ages have ever gone. In that nine month experience He showed me that 90 percent more or less of the true born again believers have no idea of what it is to walk in heavenly places in Christ (in the Holy Spirit). With the help of the Holy Spirit we are given the power to overcome the sinful nature that is bound in our flesh that encourages us to disobey God.

Satan found the Achilles' heel of the Church, concerning obedience, and has been viciously beating it. The Achilles' heel is **ignorance concerning the life of Christ in the Holy Spirit that God requires us to live.** God has not left His church without a voice. For, to those who seek to know Him more, "deep calling unto deep" for the place of fellowship and oneness with Him, He has taken us there, so that those who He has been able to take to that place of fellowship and oneness with Him could share it with others.

As the hart panteth after the water brooks, so panteth my soul after thee, O God.
Psalms 42:1

Deep calleth unto deep at the noise of thy waterspouts:
Psalms 42:7a

My disappointment has been that this message is so far above the majority in the church that they struggle to comprehend the simplicity of it. I have heard this statement, "ignorance is bliss", spoken by a person who was about to betray his friends. With spiritual truth, ignorance can cost us the salvation of our soul. Jesus said, if I had not come and spoken unto them, they had not had sin: but now they have no cloak for their sin (John 15:22). He who hungers and thirst after righteousness will be filled; this is true for those who hunger to know ALL about Him. He will reveal Himself, even His secrets to those who hunger. If we are not hungry He will not reveal Himself to us. **GET HUNGRY!!**

One constant in all of the seven churches of Asia Minor is the false and true believers. Each church has the spectators and the participators. The spectators of God's perfect will create trouble; the doers of God's perfect will do not. It is because of the true believers, that God is sending a message that encompasses God's reward and judgment. He has heard their prayers for revival, a voice against sin, for righteousness, and of judgment to come. Though the ministry of most of these churches had a shady existence, there were those in these churches who were true in heart about their walk with God and He addressed that fact with each church. God's call to the churches, and more specifically the individual, is **REVIVAL!!**

By 95 AD Jerusalem had already been devastated for 25 years, and many of the biological Jews scattered among the nations. False doctrine was increasingly taking a foothold in the Christian church. (This problem existed almost from the very beginning of the New Testament church; Acts through Jude gives testimony to this fact). Those who were maintaining a true uncompromising walk with Christ were travailing in prayer for REVIVAL.

God has always had a remnant of Spirit filled uncompromising Christians and Intercessors in every generation, even in the (dark) Middle Ages. Those who tried to reform the Catholic doctrine back to biblical truth were murdered as heretics, until Martin Luther of the 16th century. Although the Catholic Church tried to quiet him they were unable to, and God's attempted renewal of the Biblical church of the book of Acts.

Although the move to a full blown church Revival <u>worldwide</u> has been slow and arduous, near 500 years in coming, the past 100 years plus has been used of God to build to it, with the renewal of the power and gifts of His Holy Spirit filling increasing numbers of those accepting Him as Lord and Savior of their life throughout the world, with an insatiable hunger to know Him in the depth of His personality and character, intimacy with God. With this being true, there is still the existence of those who have only a religious experience with Christ, being fueled by the preaching of those who do not have the power of the Holy Spirit flowing through the veins of their own spirit and soul. These preachers are among those for whom the scripture 2 Timothy 3:5 is written: "Having a form of godliness, but denying the power thereof; from such turn away."

The reason God begins Revelation with His exhortation to these seven churches is the impact that the spiritual condition of "God's people", play in the fulfillment of prophecy. It is obvious that God's word to the seven churches, at the beginning of the book of Revelation, is not just a word from God to these seven churches of that era, but to all churches transcending all generations from the first word to the final word of God's revelation to Jesus, given to the Apostle John to write, being fulfilled. The warnings and praise, blessings and judgment to the churches of Asia Minor are a word for all generations.

All of the words of "the Revelation to Jesus Christ given to him by God" for His church is to all churches who profess to be Christian, and are as relevant for us today as they were for John's day, and not just to a congregation, but also to the very heart and spirit of each individual in any congregation. What was the significance of God exhorting these churches and not all of the churches of that era? I would say partly, because these seven churches are our example of what is an approved Christian lifestyle before God and what is not approved; **that, along with repentance from sin, will make us worthy of eternal life** (God's standard). The Religious, Hypocrite, and Lukewarm, will be cast out. It is those who obey God who will be accepted.

> **I beseech you therefore, brethren, by the mercies of God, that ye present your bodies a living sacrifice, holy, acceptable unto God, which is your reasonable service. And be not conformed to this world: but be ye transformed by the renewing of your mind, that ye may prove what is that good, and acceptable, and perfect, will of God.**
>
> **Romans 12:1-2**

Although we are saved by grace and faith, true faith compels use to obey God. Holiness in the sight of God is not obeying a set of written laws, legalistic DOs and DO NOTs, <u>it is obeying the dictates of His Holy Spirit</u>. For those who are led by the Spirit of God are the Sons and Daughters of God (Romans 8:14), but not without the instruction the bible gives to keep us on the right path to His perfect will for us. God does not have a "permissive will". If we are not obeying his "perfect will" we are in disobedience, and the rod of correction is forth coming.

For as many as are led by the Spirit of God, they are the sons of God.
Romans 8:14

As many as I love, I rebuke and chasten: be zealous therefore, and repent.
Revelation 3:19

For whom the Lord loveth he chasteneth, and scourgeth every son whom he receiveth.
Hebrews 12:6

But when we are judged, we are chastened of the Lord, that we should not be condemned with the world.
1 Corinthians 11:32

It is evident that there are those in the churches of Asia Minor who God specifically picks out by name or by the doctrine they teach, for a reason, for <u>all</u> scripture is given for our instruction. Even that which is written in the book of Revelation.

<u>All scripture</u> is given by inspiration of God, and is profitable for doctrine, for reproof, for correction, for instruction in righteousness: That the man of God may be perfect, thoroughly furnished unto all good works.
2 Timothy 3:16-17

There is so much information and research available about the history of the cities, these seven church bodies resided in, which it is not God's intent that I write about, except only to use anything about the history that would give added significance to what is already written in the second and third chapters of Revelation for those who will read this.

I do not claim to be a scholar about all I feel the Lord wants me to write, but it is my prayerful intent to write all He desires to be shared about His will for us, what makes us acceptable in His sight, and worthy of the abundant life now and the eternal life to come, that would be hidden in what He is saying to these seven church bodies, and initially to us as individual's. These two chapters embody the attitudes and conduct of those in these churches, that are just as active in the lives of every person who profess to be a Christian, whatever status they may fill within the title of "**foolish virgin**" or "**wise virgin**".

> **Then shall the kingdom of heaven be likened unto ten virgins, which took their lamps, and went forth to meet the bridegroom. And five of them were wise, and five were foolish. They that were foolish took their lamps, and took no oil with them: But the wise took oil in their vessels with their lamps. While the bridegroom tarried, they all slumbered and slept. And at midnight there was a cry made, Behold, the bridegroom cometh; go ye out to meet him. Then those virgins arose, and trimmed their lamps. And the foolish said unto the wise, Give us of your oil; for our lamps are gone out. But the wise answered, saying, Not so; lest there be not enough for us and you: but go ye rather to them that sell, and buy for yourselves. And while they went to buy, the bridegroom came; and they that were ready went in with him to the marriage: and the door was shut. Afterward came also the other virgins, saying Lord, Lord, open to us. But he answered and said, Verily I say unto you, I know you not. Watch therefore, for ye know neither the day nor the hour wherein the Son of man cometh.**
> **Matthew 25:1-13**

Oil is a biblical symbol of the Holy Spirit. The five foolish virgins are those who have a form of godliness (religion, not a true born-again experience), who whether aware or unaware, realizing something is not right in their relationship with God, try to pull the five wise down to their level of spiritual poverty, but the wise **did not fall** for it. The "foolish virgins" do not know what it is to be ONE with God, to fellowship with Him, nor to be filled with the power and gifts of His Holy Spirit. The "foolish virgins" do not know what it is to fight with demonic powers.

<u>Without the power of the Holy Spirit in our life we cannot become One with God, obey Him to the degree He desires of us, nor hear His voice telling us what to do and/or say from one moment to the next.</u> **Those who are led by the Spirit of God are the Sons of God,** Romans 8:14.

The foolish virgins, because of not having God's Holy Spirit in their heart, which produces the radical life changing born-again experience, had no oil. These are the Religious, [those who went through the ritual of repentance, without experiencing the new birth], who did not cultivate an intimate relationship with the bridegroom, causing them to have no oil, that when He did come, their lamp would not light. It is to the shame of the wise virgins that they had also allowed their flame to go out and as did the foolish virgins, also slept, but it was only to their credit that they still had oil and were able to light their lamp again. Many of us, who are filled with the power and gifts of the Holy Spirit, live out our life with Christ caught up in the responsibilities of this life to the point that the lack of "meaningful time" we need to spend with Him, causes our "walk" with Him to stagnate [liken to that of slumber] rather than be consistently developing into a deeper and more passionate love affair. This is what was happening to the Christians in the church of Ephesus, their time was being caught up it the affairs of ministry.

We are responsible for our flame; making time to spend with Him should always be our priority, not our temporal responsibilities of life. God knows we have temporal responsibilities. We all have been created with various types of talents and abilities, many of which will never be brought to full fruition unless we are totally surrendered to His "perfect will" for our life. God wants us to always be in a **"spiritual state of readiness"** to change our plans, so that when He speaks to us, we immediately do as He says. Foolish virgins are not in this condition only the wise virgins are. While God has afforded our every waking moment to glorify Him, He has special moments in time when He wants to use us for a significant "God moment."

> **But ye, brethren, are not in darkness, that that day should overtake you as a thief. Ye are all the children of light, and the children of the day: we are not of the night, nor of darkness. Therefore let us not sleep, as do others; but let us watch and be sober. For they that sleep sleep in the night; and they that be drunken are drunken in the night. But let us, who are of**

**the day, be sober putting on the breastplate of faith and love;
and for a helmet, the hope of salvation.**
1 Thessalonians 5:4-8

**Preach the word; be instant in season, out of season; reprove,
rebuke, exhort with all longsuffering and doctrine.**
2 Timothy 4:2

These are the days of Revival when God is waking up those in the church, who are among the wise virgins, to rekindle an intimate relationship with the One who loves them. I call this rising up to "Revival Status." It behooves us to encourage the born-again believers, who do not have His power and gifts in their life, to receive the baptism of the Holy Spirit.

How important is intimacy with God? It appears from the parable of the foolish and wise virgins there is some significance to it, of being worthy or not to enter into the marriage. He said: **Verily I say unto you, I know you not.** The statement **"Watch therefore"** means, <u>being vigilant to keep our lamps burning not to let the flame go out; cultivating a passionate love relationship with Him is "watching."</u> It is obvious to me that God's primary love language is "meaningful time."

<u>**To them who by patient continuance in well doing**</u> **seek for glory and honour and immortality,** <u>**eternal life: But unto them that are contentious, and do not obey the truth,**</u> **but obey unrighteousness,** <u>**indignation and wrath,**</u> **Tribulation and anguish, upon every soul of man that doeth evil;... But glory, honour, and peace, to every man that worketh good; ...**
Romans 2:7-10

"Life is what we make it", to some extent this is true with life in the Holy Spirit. For a person who is truly filled with the Holy Spirit, the endowment of power, and the gifts, to stand back and say, "Well, I have my ticket so that is all that matters," is not enough to satisfy their soul. We are compelled to leave the basics of salvation and to go on to perfection (*Hebrews 6:1-2*); the perfection that is wrapped up in striving to obey **all** of God's expectation for our life, why we were born, and the "calling" that God has created us to fulfill.

Those who say they have experienced the salvation of their soul, then not strive to obey God's perfect will, (to obey perfectly His every word, desire, and ambition), do nothing but get in the way of God's plan and could possibly fall into the category of "the foolish virgin", who though they may have a form of godliness, have no power against sin. They show by there very conduct that they are "lukewarm". These know very little of God's word and the work of the Holy Spirit, who not like the Berea Christians [Acts 17:10-11] who searched the scriptures daily to see if what Paul said was true, have very little knowledge of what is written in the Word of God. Their knowledge of the scriptures is fragmented at best, and they live a defeated life, instead of a victorious one. The Lukewarm Believer, just like the Religious and the Hypocrite will be cast out of God's presence. For as God said, "I will spue (spit) them out..." Revelation 3:16

Why continue to let the Enemy keep you bound in a life of worldliness and carnality, when God has provided through the infilling of the power of the Holy Spirit the way of escape and **the leap forward** to intimate fellowship with God in the throne room of His presence, the heavenly places in Christ, that can only be accessed with the help of the Holy Spirit? If you do not have the Holy Spirit, the endowment of power, and the gifts of the Holy Spirit being manifest in and through your life, **do not let the lies of the "foolish virgins" who choose not to believe what His word says,** keep you from the victory, power, and intimate relationship God wants to have with you, and requires. Ask Him to fill you with the power of His Holy Spirit. Don't be one of the foolish virgins who were not allowed to enter into the marriage. "**Afterward came also the other virgins, saying, Lord, Lord, open to us. But he answered and said; Verily I say unto you, I know you not.**" Matthew 25:11-12

> **And the fire upon the altar shall be burning in it; it shall not be put out: and the priest shall burn wood on it every morning, and lay the burnt offering in order upon it; and he shall burn thereon the fat of the peace offerings. The fire shall ever be burning upon the altar; it shall never go out.**
> **Leviticus 6:12-13**

It is God's desire that the fire of His presence never go out in our heart, and that it would always be burning. We are responsible for our own fire, not someone else. We are to be instant in season and out of season (2 *Tim.* 4:2), always ready to be used by God, to accomplish His will and to glorify Him by our readiness to be used, not only with His word, but also with His power and the gifts. <u>The Fire shall ever be burning and it shall never go out</u>. Being worldly and carnal, instead of always vigilant, causes the fire to go out, (the foolish virgins and the wise are an example).

The Holy Spirit keeps our flame burning. For lack of the Holy Spirit in their life, many who profess to be a Christian fall by the "way side", if ever, never to serve the Lord again. The endowment of power, which comes with the "Baptism of the Holy Spirit" is for service and helps us to have intimacy with God, which also all of the gifts of the Holy Spirit spoken of in 1 Corinthians chapter 14 are attached, gives us the ability to maintain our flame.

It has never been God's plan that the Gifts of the Holy Spirit cease in His church, but rather to continue until the coming of Jesus for His bride (the church), 1 Corinthians 1:4-8. The Gifts of the Holy Spirit have always been a manifestation of His power and presence in the lives of His people. When we are caught up in worldliness and the satisfying of carnal desire the Gifts will not flow through us, and neither will we have the fellowship our Father wants to have with us.

> **I thank my God always on your behalf, for the grace of God which is given you by Jesus Christ; That in every thing ye are enriched by him, in all utterance, and in all knowledge; Even as the testimony of Christ was confirmed in you: <u>So that ye come behind in no gift; waiting for the coming of our Lord Jesus Christ</u>: Who shall also confirm you unto the end, that ye may be blameless in the day of our Lord Jesus Christ.**
>
> **1 Corinthians 1:4-8**

Worldliness and carnal pursuits have been a problem in the church for centuries, thus causing the Gifts to become almost none existent. It is because of this that it has been believed by some that the Gifts ceased after the death of the Apostle John. There is historical proof that the Gifts where still evident into at least the fourth century AD. When our fellowship is with the Father and not with the world we are candidates for His Gifts to flow through our lives. 1 Corinthians 13:8-

13 is misinterpreted to believe that the gifts ceased when the written word became a collective work. The context is in reference to when God's plan for the church has been perfected or completed, "...then shall I know even as also I am known, v.12." 1 Corinthians 13:12 helps to understand what 1 Corinthians 13:10 means.

After God's exhortations to the churches of Asia Minor, God begins the prophetic word to the New Testament church age leading to the Rapture and Judgment seat of Christ, the reign of Antichrist, Jesus' 1000 year reign, and the great White Throne Judgment. God does not want us to get bogged down with John's description of what he saw, missing what God's desire is for His Church and another attempt to reveal Himself to us, His personality and character manifested even in the book of Revelation, His love and desire for our fellowship, unstained and unrestrained by disobedience, lukewarmness, hypocrisy, worldliness, carnality, and all forms of immorality. God's exhortation to His church <u>to obey His expectations and standard of holiness</u> is vital to the fulfillment of the time line of events laid out in the book of Revelation. Not only is the book of Revelation words of things to come, it is also a book of exhortation to challenge the Christian to **BE VIGILANT** (watching, obeying Him).

God's plan for this earth and humanity, as a whole, will be fulfilled despite our lack of obedience, but **He does not want to leave any of us, who profess to "know" him, out of His eternal plan.** Although God is longsuffering not willing that any would perish, there is still a limitation to how long He will wait. God's desires will be fulfilled despite us, even if it means removing us out of the way through death. God said this to the church of Ephesus: [Rev 2:4] **Nevertheless I have somewhat against thee, because thou hast left thy first love:**

> **Remember therefore from whence thou art fallen, and repent, and do the first works; or else I will come unto thee quickly, and <u>will remove thy candlestick out of his place</u>, except thou repent.**
>
> **Revelation 2:5**

It appears that these young Christian churches were being deceived in believing worldliness, carnality, and sexual immorality were acceptable for a Christian to practice, contradicting what "Thus says the Lord".

15

The Holy Spirit will not dwell in the church that teaches and practices worldliness, carnality, and sexual immorality, nor will He dwell in the individual Believer who does. The <u>doctrine of the Nicolaitans</u> [to be written about later] still exists today in the form of Liberalism. Here is a statement found in the chapter titled "Prophets":

"I am of the persuasion that a person who calls themselves a Christian and cusses like a sinner and behaves like one, if they truly are a Christian, does so because they are not filled with the power of the Holy Spirit to live and behave any other way; Without the power of the Holy Spirit we can never live the "Standard" that God desires for us."

Without the power of the Holy Spirit we can never live the standard of holiness God requires and expects of us. It is without His power to live according to His standard, that has caused doctrines [false doctrines found a place in some of the churches of Asia Minor] to arise **that cause those who do not possess God's power, to create a standard of holiness that they can walk in, calling it "God's permissive will"; A standard of holiness that is according to a relaxed moral code which is far below what God requires, "His perfect will".** God calls those who live according to a "relaxed moral code", workers of iniquity (lawless). The doctrine of Balaam, the doctrine of the Nicolaitans, and the doctrine of Jezebel fall into this category. Heaven will not be their eternal home, **living God's standard of holiness is <u>required not an option</u>.** God's grace is not a virtue that causes Him to be blind to rebellion, and neither is His mercy and longsuffering.

Without the power of the Holy Spirit it is impossible to live God's standard of holiness. Anyone who does not endeavor to live according to God's standard of holiness, are following the deeds and doctrine of the Nicolaitans, (Liberalism). Teaching that worldliness is an acceptable lifestyle for a Christian is a doctrine Satan has used to cause many who have made a decision to serve the Lord, to be powerless against him.

God gives the Holy Spirit to those <u>who strongly desire to obey Him</u>, a "Christian" who lives in worldliness is in disobedience, and therefore not a candidate to receive this baptism from God, but rather are subject to the judgment of God against them as were many of the churches. If they do not repent, and serve God according to His standard of holiness, the judgment of God will be on them. The Lord has shown me that all

16

of these churches had those who longed for revival, and that God was using John to let them know what was preventing revival along with the judgment if they did not repent of their disobedience, and the blessing if they did repent. God gives the Gift of the Holy Spirit to those who desire to please (obey) Him.

And we are his witnesses of these things; and so is also the Holy Ghost, whom God hath given to them that obey him.

Acts 5:32

I would tend to believe that 2 Peter 2:1 is a very good synoptic overview of the type of people who pedaled the doctrine of the Nicolaitans, the doctrine of Balaam, and the doctrine of Jezebel.

But there were false prophets also among the people, even as there shall be false teachers among you, who privily shall bring in damnable heresies, even denying the Lord that bought them, and bring upon themselves swift destruction.

2 Peter 2:1

It is asserted by researchers of these sects that the doctrines were similar. Here are key words: (a false freedom or licentiousness), (a disregard for holy living), (encouraged a return to pagan laxity of morals), (taught that Christian liberty meant license to commit sensual sins), (supported by a "doctrine," accompanied by the boast of a prophetic illumination, (Jezebel) [a word of prophecy, which was not from God.]).

Faith to believe there is a God is not saving faith, (*devils believe and tremble, James 2:19*) this faith just acknowledges that there is a Creator; it does not make Him our Father. This was the kind of faith **Simon of Samaria Acts 8:9-24, and Jezebel of Thyatira Rev 2:20-22** had. They went through the motion or ritual of repentance, but obviously did not have a true and sincere heart of repentance. They did not experience the "new birth", the sinful nature being replaced by the righteous nature of God.

Simon and Jezebel believed the report about the true God, but only received a religious experience, not a true life changed born again experience with Christ, the Apostle acknowledged this concerning Simon (*Acts 8:23*). Jesus said to the Pharisees and Sadducees that you are of your father the devil (John 8:44). These were the "elite" religious leaders, "religious" being the key word. They had a form of godliness, *(do as they say not as they do, Matt. 23:3-5)*, but not the life changing experience that <u>saving faith </u>provides. Saving faith that not only acknowledges God is our Creator, but that makes Him our Father also.

Saving faith compels us to obey God with all of our heart, mind, soul, and strength *(Mark 12:30-33, Luke 10:27)*, the faith that causes us to abhor sin and avoid it. This faith causes us <u>not </u>to be partakers of other men's sin *(1 Tim. 5:22)*. Our contact with Sinners is for their conversion to Christ, not to be partaker of their sin. Light and darkness cannot have fellowship *(2 Cor. 6:14,17-18)*. Primary association with Sinners will cause us to become lax in our Christ-like values and eventually lead to backsliding, forsaking the Lord altogether, falling back into the sinful lifestyle the Lord delivered us from to serve Him and to receive eternal life in the last day of our life *(1 Peter 1:5,9)*.

Who are kept by the power of God through faith unto salvation ready to be revealed in the last time...Receiving the end of your faith, even the salvation of your souls.
1 Peter 1:5, 9

He who endures to the end shall be saved *(Matt. 10:22)*, not he who walks with the Lord for a while then returns to a sinful lifestyle *(choke the word, Mark 4:19, Luke 8:14)*. Salvation is what we receive at the end of our days *(1 Peter 1:5)*; saving faith in the present is the "down payment", "earnest money" *(Eph 1:14; 2 Cor. 1:22, 5:5)*, for the promise of salvation. When we take back the "deposit", God takes back the "promise" and blots our name out of the book of life. Revelation 3:5, this is one reference, which states blotting out our name can happen. This one scripture among others *(Exodus 32:32-33, Rev 22:19)* makes the "once saved always saved" and "eternal security" doctrine incorrect theology, which in itself has only been around about five hundred years, a doctrine the Apostles never taught.

As long as we are maintaining a "saving faith" walk with God, God's promise of the salvation of our soul in our last day is "secure". If we commit a sin, that does not destroy our "saving faith", for if any man sin we have an advocate with the Father, Jesus Christ (1 John 2:4). Bare in mine the scripture says "<u>IF</u> ANY MAN SIN", implying that sin is not to be our common practice, I stated earlier that "saving faith" compels us to obey God *(Romans 3:31)*, without "saving faith" we will continue in habitual sinfulness, and only have a "religious experience" with an unchanged sinful nature, then at the end of our life receive the judgment of eternal damnation, not eternal life, [*patient continuance in well doing... Romans 2:7*]

The reference in Exodus 32:32-33 is believed, because of the Hebrew meaning of the word, to imply that the Old Testament's use of the book of life (book of the living) is in reference to those presently living, while in the New Testament the meaning is in reference to eternity. If the name were removed God would send immediate judgment on the individual or individuals, those in the Old Testament. When God said to Moses, ...whosoever has sinned against me, him will I blot out of my book, the Hebrew meaning of the word "sinned" means: habitual sin. So more correctly... whosoever sins against me habitually, him will I blot out of my book.

Obviously, whatever the use of the wording, whether Old or New Testament, those who sin habitually will be blotted out of the Book of Life. Those who have given their heart to Christ do not fall into the category of the habitual sinner. For though we may commit sin, *yielding to the desire of the sinful nature in our flesh,* it is not in our "new nature," *placed in the inner man* to sin habitually. A "Backslider", the person who forsakes the Lord and returns to their old lifestyle, falls into the category of "the habitual sinner", as well as the person who has never given their heart to Christ. The backslider does not fall into the category of "He that overcomes", and "He that endures to the end" *(Matthews 10:22)*. Therefore the backslider's name will be blotted out of the book of life. **Yet, all of their remaining days, God will work with them in an effort to restore them to Him self, and reestablish His favor in their life.**

Jesus said there are those who will stand in the Judgment, saying did we not cast out devils in your name...? The Lord said, depart from me you workers of iniquity I never knew you [Matthew 7:23, Luke 13:27]. For years I questioned that statement, for it made those who have the gifts of the Holy Spirit appear to be unaccepted by God. The Lord showed me that what caused them to be rejected was those deeds were past tense in their lives, for they at one time did obey Him and have an intimate relationship with Him, so He could use them to do great wonders for His glory, but sometime before their death they had stopped obeying

Him and being intimate with Him, they were backslidden. Therefore when they said that bold statement to Him, He said I do not know you. They were cast out of His presence. They were in a backslidden condition, and their name was not in the Book of Life.

And whosoever was not found written in the book of life was cast into the lake of fire.
Revelation 20:15

In the Old Testament, God asked the children of Israel, if a man turns to serve Him, then turns back, will his righteousness be remember? The answer of God was, No it will not *(Ezekiel 33:11-19)*. If I were to forsake the Lord (backslide), all of the treasure I have stored up in heaven will be lost, and I will fall under the same judgment of God against those who have rejected Him all of the days of their life. My name would be blotted out of the Book of Life and I will spend eternity in hell instead of in His presence. For both Old and New testaments speak of our name can be "blotted out". **A person who professes to be a Christian can justify their sin all they want, it is a device of the Enemy to keep them trapped, unusable, and of very little value to God**, then in the last day of their life, when they enter eternity and stand before God, He may say "depart from me, you worker of iniquity I never knew you," rather than "enter thou into the joy of the Lord thou good and faithful servant."

"Not everyone is meant to have the gift of the Holy Spirit" (God's power and gifts), is a lie of the Enemy to keep a "Christian" <u>powerless</u> against him and trapped in a sinful pattern of living, and with this behavior a fearful looking of fiery indignation that will devour God's adversaries.

For if we sin willfully after that we have received the knowledge of the truth, there remaineth no more sacrifice for sins, But a certain fearful looking for of judgment and fiery indignation, which shall devour the adversaries.
Hebrews 10:26-27

Let us therefore fear, lest, a promise being left us of entering into his rest, any of you should seem to come short of it.
Hebrews 4:1

Brethren, if any of you do err from the truth, and one convert him; Let him know, that he which converteth the sinner from the error of his way shall save a soul from death, and shall hide a multitude of sins.

James 5:19-20

Chapter 2
– Grace –

[*The grace of God is used interchangeably to include many different aspects of His attitude, character, and work for the salvation of our soul and to establish and build our relationship with Him. What will follow is to clarify two of the aspects of His "grace".*]

For by grace are ye saved through faith; and that not of yourselves: it is the gift of God: Not of works, lest any man should boast.

Ephesians 2:8-9

It is true that we are saved by grace through faith and that there is nothing we can do, no good moral deed, nor anything that could merit salvation on our part. There is nothing that we can do that would cause God to pardon our sin and grant us access to eternal life, for the exception of repenting of our sin to accept God's gift of salvation, this God has established to be a fact. Good works do not save us, but holy living or more specifically, obedience to God's perfect will for our life, His every desire which He speaks to us being fulfilled, <u>after repentance</u>, guarantees the salvation of our soul through and by grace and faith when we pass from this life. **Not only does the grace of God save us, His grace also teaches us to obey Him.** [Titus 2:11-13]

If after having received God's promise of eternal life by grace through faith, out of a sincere and true heart, we do not go onto perfection [the perfecting work that God requires to be manifested in and through our flesh, that righteous nature that He has engrafted in our spirit working in and through our flesh, to cause the righteous nature of God that is in our spirit to be seen by the way we live] we will be in jeopardy of being denied eternal life. More simply stated, **works do not save us, but obedience to God's perfect will keeps us within the promise of salvation** *[psalms 91:1,4]*. Continuing in worldly and carnal behavior, after presumably accepting Jesus as Lord and Savoir of our life, in God's sight is rebellion. <u>Continuing in worldly and carnal behavior **is** rebellion</u>.

> <u>**Therefore leaving the principles of the doctrine of Christ, let us go on unto perfection;**</u> **not laying again the foundation of repentance from dead works, and of faith toward God, Of the doctrine of baptisms, and of laying on of hands, and of resurrection of the dead, and of eternal judgment.**
>
> **Hebrews 6:1-2**

It is rebellion to God's will that caused Adam and Eve's fall from grace, and the righteous nature of God that they were created with to be replaced by a sinful nature. **The righteous nature of God, in those of us who are truly born again, compels us to live a wholly obedient life to do the perfect will of God.** This is what "going onto perfection" means: The perfection that is in our spirit being manifested in our flesh.

This desire of God can be a life long process, but He does require it and has made it a predestinated law that is a part of the promise of the salvation of our soul. God has made it a supernatural fact that our life is to be an example of Jesus to the "world." If a person cannot tell the difference between a Sinner, and us there is a definite fault, and the fault is not God's it is ours. **God has provided everything necessary to overcome the sinful nature** that is bound in our "flesh", **through the power of the Holy Spirit.** Just as Jesus was able to resist all temptation, God has made it possible for us to resist all temptation also, through the power of the Holy Spirit.

> **According as <u>his divine power hath given unto us all things</u> that pertain unto life and godliness, through the knowledge of him that hath called us to glory and virtue:**
>
> **2 Peter 1:3**

For the grace of God that bringeth salvation hath appeared to all men, Teaching us that, denying ungodliness and worldly lusts, we should live soberly, righteously, and godly, in this present world; Looking for that blessed hope, and the glorious appearing of the great God and our Saviour Jesus Christ;

Titus 2:11-13

For whom he did foreknow, he also did predestinate to be conformed to the image of his Son, that he might be the firstborn among many brethren.

Romans 8:29

<u>Therefore leaving the principles of the doctrine of Christ, let us go on unto perfection;</u> not laying again the foundation of repentance from dead works, and of faith toward God, Of the doctrine of baptisms, and of laying on of hands, and of resurrection of the dead, and of eternal judgment. And this will we do, if God permit. For it is impossible for those who were once enlightened, and have tasted of the heavenly gift, and were made partakers of the Holy Ghost, And have tasted the good word of God, and the powers of the world to come, If they shall fall away, to renew them again unto repentance; seeing they crucify to themselves the Son of God afresh, and put him to an open shame. For the earth which drinketh in the rain that cometh oft upon it, and bringeth forth herbs meet for them by whom it is dressed, receiveth blessing from God: <u>But that which beareth thorns and briers is rejected, and is nigh unto cursing; whose end is to be burned.</u>

Hebrews 6:1-8

CHAPTER 3
- E P H E S U S -

Unto the angel of the church of Ephesus write; These things saith he that holdeth the seven stars in his hand, who walketh in the midst of the seven golden candlesticks; I know thy works, and thy labour, and thy patience, and how thou canst not bear them which are evil: and thou hast tried them which say they are apostles, and are not, and hast found them liars: And hast bourne, and hast patience, and for my names's sake hast laboured, and hast not fainted. Nevertheless I have somewhat against thee, because thou hast left thy first love. Remember therefore from whence thou art fallen, and repent, and do the first works; or else I will come unto thee quickly, and will remove thy candlestick out of his place, except thou repent. But this thou hast, that thou hatest the deeds of the Nicolaitanes, which I also hate. He that hath an ear, let him hear what the Spirit saith unto the churches; To him that overcometh will I give to eat of the tree of life, which is in the midst of the paradise of God.

Revelation 2:1-7

[*The Lord walks in the midst of the candlesticks (churches), this also speaks of His Holy Spirit's presence in our life, our soul, our spirit. (Love the Lord with all thy heart, soul, mind, strength...Mark 12:30).*]

Revelation 2:1

Unto the angel [*Pastor*] **of the church of Ephesus** [*desirable*] **write;**

These things saith he that holdeth the seven stars [*Pastors, ch. 1:20*] **in his right hand,**

who walketh in the midst of the seven golden candlesticks [*churches, Rev 1:20*]

[*GOD SAW THEIR HEART DESIRE TO BE FAITHFUL TO OBEY THE GREAT COMMISSION...*]

2:2

I know thy works, [*Gk: deeds, good works*]

and thy labour, [*Gk: obedience, intense labor, united with trouble, toil, sorrow, grief, weariness; intercession*]

and thy patience, [*Gk: loyalty to the faith, steadfastness, perseverance, and piety*]

and how thou canst not bear them which are evil: [*have no desire for the lifestyle of the unsaved*]

and thou hast tried them which say they are apostles, and are not, and hast found them liars:

[*False apostles: Ministers of Satan and not from God, who encouraged sin instead of holiness...2 Corinthians 11:13-15, Acts 20:28-30. These may be the ones who were trying to deceive the Ephesian Christians to follow the doctrine or deeds of the Nicolaitans - v.6, a doctrine whether exactly that or in the form of another title like Baal worship, etc. that a few of the churches had fallen prey to.*]

2:3 [*GOD SAYS HE SEES THEY ARE BEING FAITHFUL TO FULFILL THE GREAT COMMISSION...*

And hast borne, [*Gk: To carry a load, burden, sustain, uphold, support*] and hast patience, [Gk: *loyalty to faith, steadfastness, perseverance, and piety*]

and for my name's sake hast laboured, [Gk: *wearisome effort, toil, physical labor*]

and hast not fainted. [Gk: *have not grown weary, tireless*]

2:4

Nevertheless I have somewhat against thee, because thou hast left thy first love.

2:5

Remember therefore from whence thou art fallen [Gk. *fallen powerless, fallen away*],

and repent, and do the first works; or I will come unto thee quickly, and will

remove thy candlestick [*church*] out of his place, except thou repent.

2:6

But this thou hast, that. thou hatest the deeds of the Nicolaitans, which I also hate

2:7

He that hath an ear, let him hear what the Spirit saith unto the churches [*he who has spiritual understanding*]

To him that overcometh will I give to eat of the tree of life, which is in the midst of the paradise of God.

The Ephesian Christians did all of the right things, not just desiring to fulfill the great commission "to go into all the world", they were very passionately doing it, but in all of their being busy, their intimacy with God was compromised. God wants more than acts of service, adoration, gift giving, and physical touch, He wants meaningful time (intimacy, fellowship). **The more meaningful time we spend with Him, He brings us into a deeper fellowship with Himself, which produces a greater anointing in our life to be more effective for Him and to take us into the fulfilling of our individual "callings".** Why should God reveal our "calling" to us, without the Holy Spirit we cannot fulfill it. If we can't obey Him now or won't obey Him it is needless for Him to tell us. Do you want to know your "calling", "God's will for your life", become intimate with Him, develop the love relationship that encompasses "meaningful time". The Holy Spirit is the one who brings us to this. Worshiping in spirit and in truth, is not just the act of praising, it is also a relationship bound in fellowship and intimacy with God.

God had no problem with their laboring to get the message of salvation to as many as they could, actually He commends them, but here God is trying to get their attention about something necessary to be an effective witness and testimony for Him to lost souls. **All of the efforts to win souls for Christ produce very little results, without His anointing.** Paul said about himself, "But I keep under my body, and bring it into subjection: lest that by any means, when I have preached to others, I myself should be a castaway (Hebrews 6:8 translates the same Greek word [AAdmivn] as, **rejected**)." 1 Corinthians 9:27.

In order to be an effective, efficient, anointed, and powerful testimony for Christ we need to be consistent with spending "meaningful time" with Him, through daily bible study, prayer, and worship, regular fasting from meals if not daily, no less than weekly, fellowshipping with other Christians to share new revelations God has given to each of us, and attending the corporate gathering of other believers (church attendance). Doing these things help to keep us, "instant in season and out of season," and help us to have a more keen sense of spiritual hearing, then when God speaks to us we can confidently know it is Him speaking. We are responsible for our own flame and candlestick, neglecting what is necessary to keep it burning will cause it to go out, and our candlestick to be removed, v.5.

Jesus did nothing, nor said anything, unless the Father told Him to do it (John 8:28-29). It is with this discipline, that made it possible for Jesus to do and say things that produced awesome results in the life of everyone whose path He crossed and whose path crossed His. Every encounter with anyone was an <u>anointed</u> "God moment", no matter if He was speaking to religious hypocrites or with those individuals who sincerely wanted what He came to give. The Apostles learned the principle of obeying God, which helped to give them the ability to clearly hear Him speak to them, and be effectively used by God to "turn the world upside down", (Acts 17:6).

If I am somewhere God has not told me to be, I am in disobedience, for if I am somewhere I am not suppose to be, this means I am suppose to be somewhere else. I have come to believe that whether through a "direct word from God" or a "providential circumstance", that God initiates, no matter where I go or what I do, it is a potential God moment for me, and it is so for all of us who are true Saints. There are many examples of a "providential circumstance"; I will provide one: I need to go to the store to buy some groceries, on my way, instead of going to a local store; I decide to drive to a more distant one, my preference? No. It could be a "God moment" that I am unaware of until I get to that store, then my path and someone else cross and God says, speak to them. I did not know that when I left the house that that occasion would happen, but through a "providential circumstance" that person and I meet for a "God moment". A "direct word from God" would be, Samuel I want you to get up right now and go to Kroger for there is someone I want you to lead to repentance. This is what God did with Philip and the Ethiopian eunuch (Acts 8:26,29).

Without the baptism of the Holy Spirit (the infilling of the power and gifts), it is like standing outside looking in; the supernatural abundances of God are only seen and questioned instead of received and understood. For a "Christian" to ask, "How do you know when God is speaking to you," it is a pretty good possibility they have not cultivated an intimate love relationship with Him? The same is true if they say; "God does not speak to His people anymore." I asked one person who said that, how did you know you were a sinner in need of a Savior, He said, God told me. I asked then you are saying that God speaks to sinners but not to His people?

The only way I can know what house or car to buy, what church to attend, what job I am to have, the one I am to marry, or any life altering decision is for God to speak to me and let me know. If His Holy Spirit does not lead us we are not His people *(Roman 8:14)*. Those who are led by the Spirit of God are the children of God. Yet, one well known theologian of years past said, After the last Apostle the need to ask for the Holy Spirit is no longer necessary; that statement was so wrong and was from Satan not God.

If I have not adequately cultivated a "love relationship" with my Father, when He speaks to me, I will not hear Him, or if I do hear Him I will be in doubt if He is speaking. The Ephesian Christians where making the plans for the fulfillment of the "Great Commission" but neglecting to seek God's guidance where to go or who to speak to. Somewhere along the way they had neglected to pray for God to lead them. <u>Our "first love" is the desire to obey and spend meaningful time with Him</u>. **The Ephesian Christians had gotten so busy that they neglected the more important thing about their life, soul, and love relationship with God, <u>intimacy with Him</u>** (*Read the account of what Jesus said of Mary to Martha in Luke 10:39-42. Mary, who sat at Jesus' feet, But one thing is needful: and Mary hath chosen that good part, which shall not be taken away from her*). The name Ephesus means "desirable". Neglecting intimacy with God causes us to become undesirable. The "church" is a love relationship with God; for, we are His Bride (*John 3:29*).

When we are in love with someone, we want to know everything about them, we want to spend our every waking moment with them, we want to touch and hold them, their every desire is "our command", and we are always saying nothing but good things to others about them. This is the example of first love toward God as well.

Asia minor was a cesspool of idolatry and all kinds of doctrines from demonic sources. Although Ephesus was actively fulfilling the "Great Commission", they were allowing their lack of love relationship (intimacy with God) to put them in a compromising position for false doctrines, something many of the other churches fell prey to. Lukewarmness opens a church and the individual Christian up for the possible infiltration of false doctrines or a laxity of morals, that which the doctrine of the Nicolaitans promoted.

The Lord said to the Ephesian Christians, when having left their first love, **"Remember therefore from whence thou art fallen, and repent.** The Greek word for "fallen" [ejkphdavw] means: fallen, to <u>fall powerless</u>, to fall off of, to <u>fall away</u>. With this definition, to say "backslidden" is not a stretch of the word, therefore God says, "repent". The loss of their first love put them in a fallen powerless condition, they needed to rekindle their first love. To "do the first works" is to do that which causes a fervent love relationship to develop to what it once was, FERVENT! Spending meaningful time with God will rekindle the "fire." God is letting us know that if we will not neglect intimacy with Him we will overcome and receive the promised inheritance, eternal life in His presence (life in its fullness, abundant forever) and all of the blessings that are associated with it, not only in the life to come but also in this life [John 10:10].

To him that overcometh will I give to eat of the tree of life, which is in the midst of the paradise of God.
Revelation 2:7

CHAPTER 4
~ CHRISTIAN LIBERTY ~

Christian liberty is freedom to live like Jesus did in His days on earth as a man. It is liberty to live like Jesus not like the world. If we choose to live like the world, then we can expect to suffer the consequences of our "worldly" behavior.

As free, and not using your liberty for a cloke of maliciousness, but as the servants of God.

1 Peter 2:16

How others judge us is of no consequence, when it comes to eternity, it is how God judges us that matters. We know when our behavior is bringing Him glory and honor, and when it is not. If we are unsure we need to seriously ask Him, then seriously obey what He tells us.

For the name of God is blasphemed among the Gentiles (*sinners*) **through you, as it is written.**

Romans 2:24

Within about the first year as a Christian I was passing out tracts on High Street in Columbus Ohio within the Ohio State campus area. It was dark at the time. There was a hand full of men within a circle talking to one another. I entered the circle and gave each of them a tract (Christian literature on how to give their heart to Jesus). After failing miserably at my first attempt to witness, after I was converted, I prayed that the Lord would always give me an answer for any question that any one would ask me about Him. I was nineteen years old.

One of the men said, I have a question for you. I said OK; the Lord will give me an answer for any question you ask. One of his friends went down a sidewalk, which was between two buildings and urinated on the wall of one of the buildings. The man pointed to his friend and asked; did he sin when he did that? All public law aside, none of which I knew anything about that act, I interpreted his question as a religious one.

As I waited for an answer from God, the man asked, Well did he? I said to him, I am waiting on an answer from God. Right as I said that, God gave me the answer. I said, yes! The man said, what?!! I said, He's a sinner, everything he does is sin, even his own righteousness is as filthy rags in the sight of God, but if I had done it, it would not have been a sin, for in God's sight I am righteous. I don't remember any more than this, but I am certain we all parted amazed. About a week later as I was reading in the book of Titus, God confirmed what I said to the man was from Him. The reference is Titus 1:15-16.

Unto the pure all things are pure: but unto them that are defiled and unbelieving is nothing pure; but even their mind and conscience is defiled. They profess that they know God; but in works they deny him, being abominable, and <u>disobedient</u>, and unto every good work reprobate.

Titus 1:15-16

God has delivered us from the bondage of sin and death to no longer be controlled by its grip. We now have a choice when once we did not. As "Sinners" when we did right, God saw it as evil. For, everything we did as Sinners was classified as sin. The fruit of the "sinful nature" is sin. As Sinners our good is as filthy rags in God's sight. God does not see any sin a Christian does as sin, but as disobedience, for God deals with us as Saints and Sons not as Sinners, therefore with disobedience comes discipline.

For the law of the Spirit of life in Christ Jesus hath made me free from the law of sin and death.

Romans 8:2

But when we are judged, we are chastened of the Lord, that
we should not be condemned with the world.

1 Corinthians. 11:32

If ye endure chastening, God dealeth with you as with sons;
for what son is he whom the father chasteneth not?

Hebrews 12:7

Whosoever is born of God doth not commit sin; for his seed
remaineth in him: and he cannot sin, because he is born of
God.

1 John 3:9

Now if I do that I would not, it is no more I that do it, but sin
that dwelleth in me.

Romans 7:20

All things are lawful unto me, but all things are not expedient:
all things are lawful for me, but I will not be brought under
the power of any.

1 Corinthians 6:12

All things are lawful for me, but all things are not expedient:
all things are lawful for me, but all things edify not.

1 Corinthians 10:23

There appears to be a "gray area" for us on an individual level, God
knows what will cause us to stumble, what is not a good testimony
concerning our walk with Him, what will cause us to backslide, therefore
we as an individual have restrictions on what we can or can not do, for
what is not clearly stated in the written Word, our guide to Christ-like
living, and how to please God. God will not give us a liberty that is clearly
forbidden by scripture. I wrote earlier, "but not without the instruction
the bible gives to keep us on the right path to His perfect will for us." Not
without his written word to guide us and to help keep us out of error.

God is the One who determines what is sin for us, not someone
else. God knows our weaknesses and strengths, what will cause us to
backslide and what will not. Judging one another on the basis of our
own weaknesses and strengths is judging in error. This is not to say that

there is therefore no boundaries concerning what is sin and what is not, for Paul emphasized that, *"All things are lawful for me, but all things are not expedient: all things are lawful for me, but all things edify not."* 1 Corinthians 10:23. Throughout the scriptures whether it was Jesus or the Apostles, definite boundaries were made for what is unacceptable behavior, and what is an acceptable lifestyle that is Christ-like behavior.

We cannot walk in blatant disobedience, in "the way of sinners," and think God will not require it of us (discipline). For, He will not let us live out our newness of life that way. Some of the ways He will discipline us is through our finances, relationships, our health, and anything else to get our attention that He requires a "high standard" of conduct or behavior.

God <u>allows</u> difficulties and bad experiences to happen to us to draw us closer to Him, not to cause us to abandon Him. God holds us accountable for the choices we make according to the desires and dictates of the sinful nature that is bound in our flesh. There are times He will have mercy, but that does not mean He is OK with our choice, eventually He will discipline us.

Anyone who says they are His then habitually behaves and lives like an unconverted Sinner, they are not Christians they are hypocrites. Although a lifestyle like that of a "Christian" is no proof of truly being born-again, truly being born-again will produce a Christ-like behavior. <u>For, true "saving faith" in God will cause us to live the standard of holiness that excels the world's concept of morality, perfection, and Christian righteousness.</u>

But when we are judged, we are chastened of the Lord, that we should not be condemned with the world.
1 Corinthians 11:32

Ye see then how that by works (*acts, deeds, labor*) **a man is justified, and not by faith only. For as the body without the spirit is dead, so faith without works is dead also.**
James 2:24, 26

Therefore if any man be in Christ, he is a new creature: old things are passed away; behold, all things are become new.
2 Corinthians 5:17

For I say unto you, That except your righteousness shall exceed the righteousness of the scribes and Pharisees, ye shall in no case enter into the kingdom of heaven.
Matthew 5:20

I do not do righteousness because I am required to, I do it because it is now my "nature" to do it, and against my "nature" to sin, in the "inner man". When we were "Sinners" in the inner man, it was our "nature" to sin and against our "nature" to do anything good. Good moral deeds do not make a Sinner a Christian, accepting Jesus as Lord and Savior does. Doing the deeds of the "flesh" (the sinful-nature still present in our flesh) has a negative impact on the salvation of our soul. It is with this fact that the mission of the Holy Spirit through faith, the mercy, grace, and longsuffering of God, instructs us how to crucify and mortify the desires of the sinful nature still bound in our "flesh," so that His righteous nature can be manifested through us.

Light and darkness cannot have fellowship. As we live out our life in Christ there is a constant war concerning this, with God's intent that we win the battle for the manifestation of righteousness and obedience, instead of sin and rebellion to flow out of our "flesh." **People should see a copy of Jesus, when they see us.** As long as we are in this physical body the tendency to yield to the sinful nature that continues to thrive in our "flesh" will compel us to disobey God. God has given us the power of the Holy Spirit to resist and get the victory over this "tendency."

Although in our spirit we cannot sin, in our flesh we can. One of the adventures of serving Christ is learning how to crucify and mortify the tendency of the flesh to sin, to let the righteousness of God that is in our "inner man" be seen in our flesh. God has made this a law of the kingdom (predestinated, established) that this will happen as our "walk" with Him develops *(Romans 8:29)*.

Jesus is our example of how it is possible for His Saints not to sin, not to disobey God. Having suffered the temptation of the flesh to disobey God, He never yielded to the temptation, which caused Him to live a fully obedient life, thus completing the work for why He took on flesh to walk among us, which made Him worthy to be the Savoir of those who walk in His example of obedience, to obey God as He did. *(Hebrews 5:9)*. The power of the Holy Spirit is what made this possible for Jesus, and what makes it possible for us, His Saints.

I find then a law, that, when I would do good, evil is present with me. For I delight in the law of God after the inward man: But I see another law in my members, warring against the law of my mind, and bringing me into captivity to the law of sin which is in my members.

Romans 7:21-23

For whom he did foreknow, he also did predestinate to be conformed to the image of his Son, that he might be the firstborn among many brethren. Moreover whom he did predestinate, them he also called: and whom he called, them he also justified: and whom he justified, them he also glorified.

Romans 8:29-30

For it became him, for whom are all things, and by whom are all things, in bringing many sons unto glory, to make the captain of their salvation perfect through sufferings.

Hebrews 2:10

Though he were a Son, yet learned he obedience by the things which he suffered; And being made perfect, he became the author of eternal salvation unto all them that obey him;

Hebrew 5:8-9

For we have not an high priest which cannot be touched with the feeling of our infirmities; but was in all points tempted like as we are, yet without sin.

Hebrews 4:15

Jesus was born through Mary with the "righteous nature" or "seed" of God; we were not born with God's righteous nature. We acquire the "righteous nature" of God when we repent of our sin out of a true and sincere heart of faith. It is because of such faith, having the righteous nature of God in our "inner man", that we become joint-heirs with Jesus and are grafted into His family tree.

And if children, then heirs; heirs of God, and joint-heirs with Christ; if so be that we suffer with him, that we may be also glorified together.

Romans 8:17

For if the first fruit be holy, the lump is also holy: and if the root be holy, so are the branches. And if some of the branches be broken off, and thou, being a wild olive tree, wert graffed in among them, and with them partakest of the root and fatness of the olive tree; Boast not against the branches. But if thou boast, thou bearest not the root, but the root thee. Thou wilt say then, The branches were broken off, that I might be graffed in. Well; because of unbelief they were broken off, and thou standest by faith. Be not highminded, but fear: For if God spared not the natural branches, take heed lest he also spare not thee.

Romans 11:16-21

It is important that we search within ourselves to see if we are truly His, for if after having "repented of our sin," the lifestyle we live has not dramatically changed, we may still yet be under the bondage of sin and not in Christ.

Examine yourselves, whether ye be in the faith; prove your own selves. Know ye not your own selves, how that Jesus Christ is in you, except ye be <u>reprobates</u> [*Castaway; Rejected; Gk: that which does not prove itself such as it ought; unfit; not approved*]?

2 Corinthians 13:5

Stand fast therefore in the liberty wherewith Christ hath made us free, and be not entangled again with the yoke of bondage.

Galatians 5:1

When my spirit has been saturated by His Holy Spirit, the "sinful nature" that was in my spirit is replaced with God's "righteous nature," putting it simply, this is being born-again. I will not walk in the way sinners, nor sit in the seat of the scornful, nor listen to the counsel of the ungodly. Rather I will follow the example of Jesus who knew no sin neither was guile found in his mouth, when He was reviled He reviled not. [1 Peter 2:22-23, Psalms 1:1]

> **Who did no sin, neither was guile found in his mouth: Who, when he was reviled, reviled not again; when he suffered, he threatened not; but committed himself to him that judgeth righteously:**
>
> **1 Peter 2:22-23**

> **Blessed is the man that walketh not in the counsel of the ungodly, nor standeth in the way of sinners, nor sitteth in the seat of the scornful.**
>
> **Psalms 1:1**

Jesus is referred to as the second Adam. For, Adam was created with the righteous nature of God in him, and Jesus had God's righteous nature from inception, God being His Father. When Adam rebelled, (disobeyed God) the righteous nature of God in him died, and the sinful nature took its place. The sinful nature and death was pasted on through the bloodline to the generations that followed. Had Jesus' father been a man, Jesus would not have been born with God's righteous nature.

> **And so it is written, The first man Adam was made a living soul; the last Adam was made a quickening spirit.**
>
> **1 Corinthians 15:45**

> **Wherefore, as by one man sin entered into the world, and death by sin; and so death passed upon all men, for that all have sinned:**
>
> **Romans 5:12**

A "Sinner" does not have the "righteous nature" of God dwelling in him only a "Saint" does. A Saint is what God calls those who are truthfully His children. We are not His children without Christ in our heart, without Jesus we are just His creation. When we are engrafted into Him, He engrafts His righteous nature into us. Jesus was the only

One ever born of woman with the "righteous nature" of God in Him for God is His Father.

Adam and Eve were created with the righteous nature of God; Jesus had it at inception. When Adam and Eve chose to rebel (disobey God), the "righteous nature" in them died and the "sinful nature" took its place, and was past on as a "blood line" to every person born from Adam to this day. When anyone backslides, returns to the sinful lifestyle from which they were delivered, the righteous nature that was placed within them dies and the sinful nature, just as in Adam, takes its place. Their way of living returns to what it was before they were redeemed. With this change, once again, is the judgment of eternal damnation looming over them.

For if we sin willfully after that we have received the knowledge of the truth, there remaineth no more sacrifice for sins, But a certain fearful looking for of judgment and fiery indignation, which shall devour the adversaries.
Hebrews 10:26-27

When we are born-again we are restored to what Adam and Eve were before they rebelled, and the fellowship Adam had with God before he disobeyed, is now ours to enjoy with God as our Father. This fellowship with God is not available to us when He is only our Creator; it is only available when He is our Father. When we are born-again God becomes our Father. The Holy Spirit is the One who gives us the new birth, and it is through Him that we have the privilege to fellowship with God, and Him with us.

All who were born before Jesus' birth and all who came after Him were and are born with the "sinful nature". When we are "born-again" God plants His "righteous nature" in us. The sinful nature dies and the righteous nature takes its place. Our having His righteous nature in us makes Him our Father and not just our Creator. We have the same status as Jesus; we are God's sons and daughters.

For both he that sanctifieth and they who are sanctified are all of one: for which cause he is not ashamed to call them brethren.
Hebrews 2:11

And what agreement hath the temple of God with idols? for
ye are the temple of the living God; as God hath said, I will
dwell in them, and walk in them; and I will be their God, and
they shall be my people. Wherefore come out from among
them, and be ye separate, saith the Lord, and touch not the
unclean thing; and I will receive you, And will be a Father
unto you, and ye shall be my sons and daughters, saith the
Lord Almighty.

2 Corinthians 6:16-18

When we reduce Christianity to the level of a religious philosophy
and experience, instead of for who God sent Jesus to be for us, it is easy
to view Him, what He said and did, as just another religion, instead of a
supernaturally changed life. Serving God is not an alternate way of living
and thinking; IT IS A CHANGED NATURE, THAT EXCELS
FAR ABOVE THAT.

Therefore if any man be in Christ, he is a new creature: old
things are passed away; behold, all things are become new.

2 Corinthians 5:17

The reason the Sinner, the Religious, and the Hypocrite cannot
understand what being a new creation in Christ is, is they have not been
"born-again". It takes the Holy Spirit to give us the "new birth." The new
birth or born-again experience is the Holy Spirit removing the "sinful
nature" that is in us and replacing it with God's "righteous nature." When
this happens we become a "new creature," on the inside.

When Jesus is reduced to just another religion, just like other religions,
it is easy to disregard what we don't agree with and say, dispensational,
that not everything the word of God says applies today. When the words
of Jesus are viewed as just another philosophy, any way of living out our
life in that philosophy is acceptable, and no punishment associated with
it, whether or not it is temporal or eternal. This is the kind of faith in God
that depends simply on intellectual knowledge, without being converted
from darkness to light, born-again. These are those who justify sin with
their own moral code (the religious, hypocrite, and lukewarm). Without
the Holy Spirit we cannot live God's standard of holiness.

We justify sin and say that God is OK with that. This is the thought pattern of what some of the Believers in the seven churches of Asia "fell" into, and which made it possible for them to be deceived by the teachings of the Nicoliatans, Balaam, and Jezebel. The spirit and teachings of such as these exists in the heart of the <u>Religious</u>, the <u>Hypocrite</u>, and the <u>Lukewarm</u> today; a liberal theology about Christian liberty that interprets what Christian liberty is not. **Christian liberty is not a license to live as we please, but rather to please God, for whom we have been born-again to do. Christian liberty is freedom to do His desires, something we did not have as "Sinners", but we do have as "Saints."**

> **For it is God which worketh in you both to will and to do of his good pleasure.**
> **Philippians 2:13**

> **For I say unto you, That except your righteousness shall exceed the righteousness of the scribes and Pharisees, ye shall in no case enter into the kingdom of heaven.**
> **Matthew 5:20**

CHAPTER 5
- S M Y R N A -

And unto the angel of the church in Smyrna write; These things saith the first and the last, which was dead, and is alive; I know thy works, and tribulation, and poverty, and I know the blasphemy of them which say they are Jews, and are not, but are the synagogue of Satan. Fear none of those things which thou shalt suffer: behold the devil shall cast some of you into prison, that ye may be tried: and ye shall have tribulation ten days: be thou faithful unto death, and I will give thee a crown of life. He that hath an ear, let him hear what the Spirit saith unto the churches; He that overcometh shall not be hurt of the second death.

Revelation 2:8-10

Revelation 2:8

And unto the angel [Pastor] of the church in **Smyrna** [*myrrh*] write; These things saith the <u>first and the last</u>, which <u>was dead, and is alive;</u>

2:9

I know thy **works,** [Gk: *physical labor to do God's work in the earth*] and **tribulation,** [Gk: *emotional and physical persecution, distresses, hard times*]

and **poverty,** [Gk: *beggary, lack of substance*] (**but thou art rich**) [*God's favor*] and I know the <u>blasphemy of them which say they are Jews,</u> and <u>are not</u>, but <u>are the synagogue of Satan.</u>

[*Blasphemy: They say they are Christian, but are actually religious with no power, dead, uncircumcised in heart. These only went through the motions of repentance but did not experience the real thing like Simon the Sorcerer in the book of Acts. They allow themselves to be pawns of Satan (deceivers who spy) to cause trouble, distress, and division, first part of v. 10. Some researchers say these are physical Jews, but the wording appears to imply a condition of the "heart or spirit", this does not exempt the possibility of physical Jews having a part in encouraging persecution, for Paul had to deal with them in certain cities he evangelized, Berea being one of those cities (Acts 17:13)*]

2:10

Fear none of those things which thou shalt suffer: [*the false Christians help create persecution that causes martyrs*]

behold, <u>the devil shall cast some of you into prison, that ye may be tried; and ye shall have tribulation ten days</u>:

be thou faithful unto death,

and **I will give thee a crown of life.** [*A martyr's crown*]

2:11

He that hath an ear, let him hear**(*spiritual understanding*)

what the Spirit saith unto the **churches;** (*plural*)

He that <u>overcometh shall not be hurt of the **second death**</u> (ref: Rev 21:8)

God did not have a reprimand for the Christians of Smyrna. In the midst of all of the false doctrines circulating throughout Asia Minor they had not found a foothold with these Christians, any more than they did in Ephesus. This is not to say that the church did not have the Sinner, Religious, Hypocrite, and Lukewarm in their congregation. It is to say that, just as with the Christians in the church of Ephesus, this body of Saints had not compromised their faith and the doctrine of Jesus, for the heresies that were being taught is some of the other churches, and circulating throughout Asia Minor.

With this fact, God is pronouncing His "Favor" on them saying in v 9: **I know thy...poverty, but thou art rich.** It is because of their passion and unwavering devotion that persecution is upon them, but with their passion is God's anointing, and a deep fellowship with Him, which causes God to say, *thou art rich.* Those who are lukewarm in their walk with Christ are making the persecution the of true Saints worse.

It seems that the number one goal of some Believers is to destroy the faithfulness and loyalty of those Saints who are not walking in the same worldly and carnal lifestyle as they are. Just as it was with the foolish virgins attempt against the wise virgins to try to get them to "fall" to their level of worldliness by asking for their oil; in essence the wise virgins said, Not so, but receive the gift of the Holy Spirit for yourselves and come up to our level of obedience and fellowship with God. God has called us to strengthen each other's faith and devotion to Christ not to destroy it.

Worldly and carnal attitudes toward other Christians are not to be a part of our walk with Christ. They are not a fruit of the righteous nature of God. I put a lot of emphasis on the "gift of the Holy Spirit", the indwelling of the power and the gifts, because of how I have seen those Believers who struggle with worldliness and carnality to be helped to overcome, if they obey the correction of the Holy Spirit as He shows them how to, and as He generates the power to do it. Those who have this greater anointing in their life excel in their walk with God. **Foolish virgins try to destroy the strength, fortitude, and resolve of wise virgins trying to get them to compromise their faith and doctrine, to descend to their level of worldliness, carnality, and blatant disobedience to the Holy Spirit.**

Smyrna, just as in all the churches, had those who for lack of devotion to God were more like spies than Christians, being use of Satan to try to create division and discord, and add to the affliction and persecution that was already being waged against the Christians who were true examples of Christ. These "false-Christians" who have a form of godliness are "wells without water, dried up, twice dead. As the day of Jesus' coming and the unveiling of Antichrist draws near the chasm between the sincere and true Christian and those who are not, is growing wider, so that it is becoming more evident who is truthfully one of God's children, and who just have a religious intellectual experience concerning the salvation that is found in Christ.

The Holy Spirit teaches us to love one another unconditionally, not to be about looking for fault, nor holding onto unforgiveness and bitterness, and not to be a person who yields to wrath, anger, clamor, slander (evil speaking), and malice. (*Ephesians 4:31, Colossians 3:8*)

> **Follow peace with all men, and holiness, without which no man shall see the Lord: Looking diligently lest any man fail of the grace of God; lest any root of bitterness springing up trouble you, and thereby many be defiled;**
> **Hebrew 12:14-15**

> **And grieve not the holy Spirit of God, whereby ye are sealed unto the day of redemption.**
> **Ephesians 4:30**

> **But the fruit of the Spirit is love, joy, peace, longsuffering, gentleness, goodness, faith, meekness, temperance: against such there is no law. And they that are Christ's have crucified the flesh with the affections and lusts (*desires*). If we live in the Spirit, let us also walk in the Spirit.**
> **Galatians 5:22-25**

> **Charity suffereth long, and is kind; charity envieth not; charity vaunteth not itself, is not puffed up, Doth not behave itself unseemly, seeketh not her own, is not easily provoked, thinketh no evil; Rejoiceth not in iniquity, but rejoiceth in the truth; Beareth**

all things, believeth all things, hopeth all things, endureth all things. Charity never faileth: *(charity: unconditional love)*
1 Corinthians 13:4-8a

Be ye therefore followers of God, as dear children; and walk in love, as Christ also hath loved us, and hath given himself for us an offering and a sacrifice to God for a sweetsmelling savour. But fornication, and all uncleanness, of covetousness, let it not be once named among you, as becometh saints; Neither filthiness, nor foolish talking, nor jesting, which are not convenient: but rather giving of thanks. For this ye know, that no whoremonger, nor unclean person, nor covetous man, who is an idolater, hath any inheritance in the kingdom of Christ and of God. Let no man deceive you with vain words: for because of these things cometh the wrath of God upon the children of disobedience. Be not ye therefore partakers with them. For ye were sometimes darkness, but now are ye light in the Lord: walk as children of light: (For the fruit of the Spirit is in all goodness and righteousness and truth;) Proving what is acceptable unto the Lord. And have no fellowship with the unfruitful works of darkness, but rather reprove them.
Ephesians 5:1-11

But these, as natural brute beasts, made to be taken and destroyed, speak evil of the things that they understand not; and shall utterly perish in their own corruption; And shall receive the reward of unrighteousness, as they that count it pleasure to riot in the day time. Spots they are and blemishes, sporting themselves with their own deceivings while they feast with you; These are wells without water, clouds that are carried with a tempest; to whom the mist of darkness is reserved for ever.
2 Peter 2:12-13, 17

This know also, that in the last days perilous times shall come. For men shall be lovers of their own selves, covetous, boasters, proud, blasphemers, disobedient to parents, unthankful, unholy, Without natural affection, trucebreakers, false

51

accusers, incontinent, fierce, despisers of those that are good,
Traitors, heady, highminded, lovers of pleasures more than
lovers of God; Having a form of godliness, but denying the
power thereof: from such turn away. For of this sort are they
which creep into houses, and lead captive silly women laden
with sins, led away with divers lusts, Ever learning, and never
able to come to the knowledge of the truth. Now as Jannes and
Jambres withstood Moses, so do these also resist the truth:
men of corrupt minds, reprobate concerning the faith. But
they shall proceed no further: for their folly shall be manifest
unto all men, as theirs also was. But thou hast fully known my
doctrine, manner of life, purpose, faith, longsuffering, charity,
patience, persecutions, afflictions, which came unto me at
Antioch, at Iconium, at Lystra; what persecutions I endured:
but out of them all the Lord delivered me. Yea, and all that
will live godly in Christ Jesus shall suffer persecution. But evil
men and seducers shall wax worse and worse, deceiving, and
being deceived.

2 Timothy 3:1-12

*Now as Jannes and Jambres withstood Moses, so do these also resist
the truth: men of corrupt minds, reprobate concerning the faith.*

Just as Jannes and Jambres who stirred up rebellion against Moses to
undermine his authority and effectiveness as a leader and to try to mar
his reputation, it is the same with those who are living below what God
requires of us as His children. Allowing themselves to be plants of Satan,
those who say they are Jews [*no circumcision of the heart- Romans 2:28-
29*], but are of the synagogue of Satan, to add to the persecution that is
going on outside of the church, to create distress within the church upon
the <u>faithful and true</u> Christians. **God desires depth of character**, and
requires more than what we are giving Him in the area of total surrender
of our will to do His will only.

Beloved, when I gave all diligence to write unto you of the
common salvation, it was needful for me to write unto you,
and exhort you that ye should earnestly contend for the faith
which was once delivered unto the saints. For there are certain
men crept in unawares, who were before of old ordained to

this condemnation, ungodly men, turning the grace of our God into lasciviousness, and denying the only Lord God, and our Lord Jesus Christ. Likewise also these filthy dreamers defile the flesh, despise dominion, and speak evil of dignities. But these speak evil of those things which they know not: but what they know naturally, as brute beasts, in those things they corrupt themselves. Woe unto them! for they have gone in the way of Cain, and ran greedily after the error of Balaam for reward, and perished in the gainsaying of Core. These are spots in your feasts of charity, when they feast with you, feeding themselves without fear: clouds they are without water, carried about of winds; trees whose fruit withereth, without fruit, twice dead, plucked up by the roots; Raging waves of the sea, foaming out their own shame, wandering stars, to whom is reserved the blackness of darkness for ever. These are murmurers, complainers, walking after their own lusts; and their mouth speaketh great swelling words, having men's persons in admiration because of advantage. But, beloved, remember ye the words which were spoken before of the apostles of our Lord Jesus Christ; How that they told you there should be mockers in the last time, who should walk after their own ungodly lusts. These be they who separate themselves, sensual, having not the Spirit.

Jude 1:3, 4, 8, 10-13, 16-19

It is God's desire that we be as the meaning of the name Smyrna, which is MYRRH. Myrrh was a costly perfume, also used as an antiseptic for embalming, to mask odors, and relieve pain. God desires us to be Saints, creating peace and consolation; not creating pain, strife, unrest, division, and any other fruit common to the sinful nature that abides in the flesh.

When we totally surrender our entire life to the dictates of the Holy Spirit, to please God instead of the sinful nature in our flesh, we are giving ourselves an offering and a sacrifice to God for a sweet smelling savor. God wants to be the first and the last, and our Resurrection from death unto life, Rev. 2:8. When people see us, they should see Jesus, the exact image, character and nature of our Father. This is only possible with the anointing that is placed in and on us when we receive the baptism of the Holy Spirit, the power to be witnesses not only in word but also in deed. We are to crucify the deeds of the flesh, not indulge it.

And they that are Christ's have crucified the flesh with the affections and lusts.
Galatians 5:24

And walk in love, as Christ also hath loved us, and hath given himself for us an offering and a sacrifice to God for a sweetsmelling savour (*savor*).
Ephesians 5:2

It is significant that in v.11 the second death is mentioned because of those who say they are Jews, and are not, but are of the synagogue of Satan v.9. The second death is their judgment, as well as for the Religious, Hypocrite, and Lukewarm.

But the fearful, and unbelieving, and the abominable, and murderers, and whoremongers, and sorcerers, and idolaters, and all liars, shall have their part in the lake which burneth with fire and brimstone: which is the second death.
Revelation 21:8

He that hath an ear, let him hear what the Spirit saith unto the churches; He that overcometh shall not be hurt of the second death.
Revelation 2:11

CHAPTER 6
– PREJUDICE, JUDGING, AND –
UNCONDITIONAL LOVE

In writing about the church of Smyrna, the Christian virtue of unconditional love *(charity)* was mentioned, this segment will discuss this characteristic a little further, along with statements about judging and prejudice. The Holy Spirit teaches us to love one another unconditionally, not to be about looking for fault, nor holding onto unforgiveness and bitterness, and not to be a person who yields to wrath, anger, clamor, slander (evil speaking), and malice *(Ephesians 4:31, Colossians 3:8)*.

One of the major stumbling blocks that hinder Revival is "prejudice". By prejudice I mean the tendency to judge someone in a negative way, with the judgment of any particular person being a false judgment that was based on an incorrect perception of that particular person. This type of judgment assesses a person's character by that person's personality, the way they dress, the way they express themselves in a conversation, and so many other things, that can cause an incorrect assessment of an individual. Jesus said in John 7:24; **Judge not according to the appearance, but judge righteous judgment.**

Any judging that creates prejudice or a negative attitude toward someone grieves the Holy Spirit and hinders the manifestation of "Holy Ghost Revival". I have learned that it is every ones tendency to judge them self or someone else too highly or too critically, and very rarely correctly. Paul the Apostle suffered with this from others as well, and even Jesus suffered it. Paul wrote in 1 Corinthians 4:3-4; **"But with me it is a very small thing that I should be judged of you, or of man's judgment: yea, I judge not mine own self. For I know nothing by myself; yet am I not hereby justified: but he that judgeth me is the Lord".**

I have also learned, that as a whole, we judge others using our own weaknesses and strengths rather than giving a person the "shadow of a doubt" and esteeming them more highly than ourselves. Paul goes on to write, in 1 Corinthians 4:5; **"Therefore judge nothing before the time, until the Lord come, who both will bring to light the hidden things of darkness, and will make manifest the counsels of the hearts: and then shall every man have praise of God".** Esteeming a person more highly than our self, flows out of charity, unconditional love.

In all of the years I have been saved, very few have given me this unconditional love, and in judging me have condemned me for something the Lord has extended to me the liberty to do, based on my own weaknesses and strengths, and that have to do with the fulfilling of my "calling". Since unconditional love is a "work in progress" for all of us, I have learned to be patient and forgiving, which is a fruit of unconditional love.

> **And above all things have fervent charity among yourselves:**
> **for charity shall cover the multitude of sins.**
>   **1 Peter 4:8**

Anyone who would look for "fault" in someone rather than esteeming that person more highly than themselves, does not possess the virtue of unconditional love, or at least very little of it. In 1 Corinthians 13:5 Paul writes that one of the fruits of unconditional love is, ".... thinketh no evil." We all suffer with prejudice; it is common in the church as well as without the church. Prejudice is not a fruit of the Spirit, and should not be found in "God's church" nor in the life of one who calls them self a Christian.

> **By this shall all men know that ye are my disciples, if ye have**
> **love one to another.**
>   **John 13:35**

CHAPTER 7
- PERGAMOS -

And to the angel of the church in Pergamos write; These things saith he which hath the sharp sword with two edges; I know thy works, and where thou dwellest, even wher Satan's seat is and thou holdest fast my name, and hast not denied my faith, even in those days wherein Antipas was my faithful martyr, who was slain among you, where Satan dwelleth. But I have a few things against thee, because thou hast there them the hold the doctrine of Balaam, who taught Balac to cast a stumblingblock before the children of Israel, to eat things sacrificed unto idols, and to commit fornication. So hast thou also them that hold the docrtine of the Nicolaitans, which thing I hate. Repent; or else I will come unto you quickly, and will fight against them with the sword of my mouth. He that hath an ear let him hear what the Spirit saith unto the churches; To him that overcometh will I give to eat of the hidden manna and will give him a white stone, and in the stone a new name written, which no man knoweth saving he that receiveth it.

Revelation 2:12-17

Revelation 2:12   God's Praise of Pergamos

And to the angel [Pastor] of the church in **Pergamos** [height, elevation] write; These things saith he which hath the sharp sword with two edges; (*HEB 4:12*)

[God will send a sword to Pergamos, separation and a dividing, judgment to show who is approved and who is not]

2:13

I know thy works, [acts, deeds] and where thou dwellest, even where Satan's seat is [A city full of every detestable, and foul sin; Possible Satan worship; a city of Christian persecution] and **thou holdest fast my name,** [by their lifestyle holding Him in high regard and honor]

and **hast not denied my faith,** [the faith of Jesus, *ch. 14:12*]

even in those days wherein **Antipas was my faithful martyr,** [Like Jesus a faithful and true witness even unto death]

who was slain among you, where Satan dwelleth. [It appears this city was a favorite place for Satan to abide, perhaps as was Sodom and Gomorrah] [There was also a temple believed to be there for Satan worship]

2:14 God's Disapproval of Pergamos
But I have **a few things against thee,**

because thou hast there them that hold the **doctrine of Balaam,** who taught Balac to cast a stumbling block before the children of Israel, to eat things sacrificed unto idols, and to commit fornication. [Similar to Baal worship with sexual immorality]

2:15

So hast thou also them that hold the **doctrine of the Nicolaitans, which thing I hate.**

[There are those in the church who are following the teachings of Nicolas, similar to the followers of Baal worship and the teachings of Jezebel: idol worship, eating idol sacrifices, fornication, and sexual immorality of all types] [<u>Nicolaitan means: destruction</u> <u>of people</u>]

2:16

Repent;

or else I will come unto thee quickly,

and will fight against them with the sword of my mouth. [Anointed preaching, swift reprimands, judgment, dividing, <u>and</u> <u>His sharp two-edged sword v.12</u>]

2:17

He that hath an ear, let him hear what the Spirit saith unto the **churches** (plural);

To him that<u> overcometh will I</u> **give to eat of the hidden manna** [a reserved place at His table],

and **will give him a white stone**, (a sign of acquittal, forgiveness, acceptance) and in the stone <u>a new name written</u>, which no man knoweth saving he that receiveth it. [The new name is a sign of our being special in His sight]

Pergamos was a city built on a hilltop, positioned for advantage against attack. The name Pergamos means height or elevation. Having allowed those into the church who lived according to the doctrines of Balaam and the Nicolaitans, the advantage against demonically initiated spiritual attacks was being eroded. The beginnings of the Church had an elevated report, but they would loose it if they did not do something about the problem. The city of Pergamos had temples to everything imaginable (as did the other cities), even one for Caesar worship, something common throughout the Roman Empire. (*Idol worship is worshiping what it represents, the demon it portrays or person*).

For the word of God is quick, and powerful, and sharper than any twoedged sword, piercing even to the dividing asunder

of soul and spirit, and of the joints and marrow, and is a discerner of the thoughts and intents of the heart.

Hebrews 4:12

The doctrines of Balaam, the Nicolaitans, and Jezebel were flourishing in Asia. The establishing of God's Church was a threat to the continuation of those doctrines, and of all other demonic doctrines. At some point those who held to these doctrines were allowed to coexist with those who held to the doctrine of Christ in the church at Pergamos. This in itself might not have been a problem except that those who were new born or weak in the faith were being persuaded to embrace the false teachings of these cults, which <u>was</u> creating a problem. Initially I would believe those who held to those doctrines were allowed to coexist in the church for the salvation of their souls, but this was not happening, I would say at least for the most part. The threat of total compromise was at the "door step" of the church.

The decision to continue to allow those into the church who would not repent and stop their participation in those doctrines was a bad choice on the part of the Pastor, just as allowing the desires of the flesh to reign in our life. Those who were being persuaded to embrace these doctrines where being deceived in believing that participating in those pagan activities was acceptable in the sight of God. The doctrine of Christian Liberty was being twisted to mean just the opposite of what the writings of the Apostles taught. (A detailed description about Christian Liberty has already been written). God commended those who were not compromising their faith for those heresies, in the midst of all the demonic activity that surrounded them, along with the persecution, and even after the martyr's death of Antipas. Antipas means "father", which could imply that this is a title and not the name of someone, which could imply a previous Pastor, if not actually a faithful Christian name Antipas.

Compromising their faith is a common problem with those who do not have the Holy Spirit <u>reigning</u> in their life. Even with having read whatever form of the written word the church at Pergamos had, there were those who were still easily deceived with heresies, as it is with those Believers who do not read the bible for themselves in these days, as a daily routine. This made it easy for a demon or Satan to come along and cast doubt on the doctrine of Christ saying, "has God really said," or "this is what God really means." Those who have a compromising walk with God are double-minded and easily swayed.

A double minded man is unstable in all his ways.
James 1:8

Draw nigh to God, and he will draw nigh to you. Cleanse your hands, ye sinners; and purify your hearts, ye double minded.
James 4:8

At the time letters, written by the Apostle Paul to Ephesus, Laodicea, and Colosse, and by many of the other Apostles, were being passed from church to church, exhorting them not to allow this to happen [Colossians 4:16]. Read the prophecy of Paul to the Ephesian Elders in Acts 20:29-30. I would say obviously this was a prophetic word for all of Asia. Just as then so it is now, there are those who by their doctrine either change the word of God, or ignore what they choose not to believe.

And from Miletus he sent to Ephesus, and called the elders of the church. And when they were come to him, he said unto them, Ye know, from the first day that I came into Asia, after what manner I have been with you at all seasons,.. For I know this, that after my departing shall grievous wolves enter in among you, not sparing the flock. Also of your own selves shall men arise, speaking perverse things, to draw away disciples after them.
Acts 20:17-18, 29-30

And when this epistle is read among you, cause that it be read also in the church of the Laodiceans; and that ye likewise read the epistle from Laodicea
Colossians 4:16

Peter, an apostle of Jesus Christ, to the strangers scattered throughout Pontus, Galatia, Cappadocia, Asia, and Bithynia, Elect according to the foreknowledge of God the Father, through sanctification of the Spirit, unto obedience and

> **sprinkling of the blood of Jesus Christ: Grace unto you, and**
> **peace, be multiplied.**
>
> **1 Peter 1:1-2**

The Greek word for "hold" in v14 and v15, **kratevw** or **krateo** has various meanings, one definition is " to have power, be powerful, to be chief, be master of, to rule. With this definition the implication is that the ones who held to those pagan doctrines could be instructors or teachers of these pagan doctrines who attended the church of Pergamos. A reason that could let this happen would be to make the church more socially acceptable to the government and the general population, causing the persecution to back off, if not cease altogether. **This is called COMPROMISE.** The Lord exposed that the underlying attempt by Satan was to use these doctrines as a stumbling block for His people v14, and as is the meaning of Nicolaitan: to destroy God's people.

Whatever the reasoning for allowing these pagan doctrines, doctrines of devil, to be influencing the church in part or as a whole, the Lord says, **REPENT, or else I will come unto thee quickly, and will fight against them with the sword of my mouth,** (expose them for the liars they are). God is threatening judgment on those who are influencing the flock to disobey Him, to compromise Christian liberty (liberty from the <u>bondage</u> of sin and death to be <u>free</u> to obey God) for worldly pleasures, and carnal behavior and conduct. The doctrine of Balaam and the Nicolaitans continue to flourish in the form of Liberalism, and as He said in v15 about this doctrine, **"which thing I hate."** God's judgment extends to any preacher, teacher, or anyone who calls themselves a Christian, who condones by their doctrine, "world" likeness and the satisfying of carnal desire, the sinful nature that is bound in the flesh, which God has told us to crucify. Those like these fall into the category of "foolish virgins."(Hypocrite, Religious, Lukewarm)

> **And they that are Christ's have crucified the flesh with the**
> **affections and lusts. If we live in the Spirit, let us also walk in**
> **the Spirit.**
>
> **Galatians 5:24-25**

> **But there were false prophets also among the people, even**
> **as there shall be false teachers among you, who privily shall**

bring in damnable heresies, even denying the Lord that bought them, and bring upon themselves swift destruction.

2 Peter 2:1

Mortify therefore your members which are upon the earth; fornication, uncleanness, inordinate affection, evil concupiscence, and covetousness, which is idolatry: For which things' sake the wrath of God cometh on the children of disobedience: In the which ye also walked some time, when ye lived in them. But now ye also put off all these; anger, wrath, malice, blasphemy, filthy communication out of your mouth. Lie not one to another, seeing that ye have put off the old man with his deeds; And have put on the new man, which is renewed in knowledge after the image of him that created him: Where there is neither Greek nor Jew, circumcision nor uncircumcision, Barbarian, Scythian, bond nor free: but Christ is all, and in all. Put on therefore, as the elect of God, holy and beloved, bowels of mercies, kindness, humbleness of mind, meekness, longsuffering; Forbearing one another, and forgiving one another, if any man have a quarrel against any: even as Christ forgave you, so also do ye. And above all these things put on charity, which is the bond of perfectness. And let the peace of God rule in your hearts, to the which also ye are called in one body; and be ye thankful. Let the word of Christ dwell in you richly in all wisdom; teaching and admonishing one another in psalms and hymns and spiritual songs, singing with grace in your hearts to the Lord. And whatsoever ye do in word or deed, do all in the name of the Lord Jesus, giving thanks to God and the Father by him.

Colossians 3:5-17

Compromising their faith is a common problem with those who do not have the Holy Spirit reigning in their life. A reason for compromise is to be popular in the church, among the congregation, and in the world with those whose father is the devil [John 8:44]. Many in the Ministry are guilty of doing this by white washing the scriptures or totally avoiding any doctrine that would create a bad report with the parishioners. God abhors this conduct. We are to preach the word in its fullness without compromise.

> **For do I now persuade men, or God? or do I seek to please men? <u>for if I yet pleased men, I should not be the servant of Christ</u>.**
> **Galatians 1:10**

> **Ye adulterers and adulteresses, <u>know ye not that the friendship of the world is enmity with God? whosoever therefore will be a friend of the world is the enemy of God</u>. Do ye think that the scripture saith in vain, The spirit that dwelleth in us lusteth to envy, But he giveth more grace. Wherefore he saith, God resisteth the proud, but giveth grace unto the humble. Submit yourselves therefore to God. Resist the devil, and he will flee from you. Draw nigh to God, and he will draw nigh to you. Cleanse your hands, ye sinners; and <u>purify your hearts, ye double minded</u>.**
> **James 4:4-8**

The Lord has given a promise to those of us who will not compromise with the "works the of flesh" and not be "partakers of other men's sins." The doctrine of Balaam and the Nicolaitans encouraged idol worship and partaking of the food sacrificed to idols. In Rev 2:17 God says, **To him that overcometh will I give to eat of the hidden manna,** this is a reserved place at His table; and **will give him a white stone,** a symbol of acquittal, forgiveness, acceptance; and in the stone **a new name written, which no man knoweth saving he that receiveth it,** <u>the new name only we would understand is an indication of our being SPECIAL in His sight</u>.

A device of the devil against those who are not compromising their walk with God is to try to bind us with depression, harboring grief and heartbreak when those who call themselves "brothers and sisters in Christ" reject us. Here is a remedy for this attack:

CHAPTER 8

– JESUS IS OUR EXAMPLE –
<u>REJECTION</u>

Jesus did not let the attitudes of the Religious of His day, among men, have a negative impact on His ability to function in His calling, His purpose for walking among us. He was despised, rejected, and afflicted, the love of God in Him caused Him to ignore that treatment, to see the inner need of those who treated Him that way. <u>Jesus did not live His life to win a popularity contest</u>. He knew why He came to us, what His mission was, and the ill treatment by others was not going to deter Him. <u>Pleasing His Father was paramount in His purpose for living among us (John 8:28-29)</u>, which God requires of us also. We cannot please man and be pleasing to God.

> **Ye adulterers and adulteresses, know ye not that the friendship of the world is enmity with (*hatred of*) God? whosoever therefore will be a friend of the world is the enemy of God.**
> **James 4:4**

Jesus did not tolerate the rejection of the religious leaders, their sanctimonious, hypocritical, "better than thou", self-righteous approach not only toward Him, but that which was directed toward others also. When Jesus was confronted by them He always exposed them for what they were in the sight of God, hypocrites, vipers, white washed sepulchers full of dead men's bones. If they did not want Him in their space, He walked away from them, unless the Father told Him to confront them. Most confrontations were not "pretty", some went away ashamed, while others went away with plans to kill Him or at least to try to discredit Him in the sight of the people.

The Lord has our testimony for Him in His hands, if so called "Christians" choose to despise and reject us, **it is not God's intention that we allow ourselves to be afflicted by that emotionally, mentally, nor physically. We are to pray for them.** Jesus said, pray for those who despitefully use you and persecute you, Matthew 5:44. **If they choose not to love us, it is to their own discredit, shame, and moral spiritual decline.** We are not to let the "Enemy" afflict us with their attitude, we are to pray for them, love them still, even if that love is not reciprocated.

A sister in Christ was told by her husband, "those who love deeply, hurt deeply". As true as this is, it is not God's will for us to hurt when we are rejected. We were created the way we are, for our "callings". Not everyone is going to be "comfortable" in our presence; it is because of that fact that they will not associate with us.

Concerning my "calling", there are those who will hear me who will not hear someone else. Some will accept me; some will reject me. When we accept this fact, we can deal with the rejection gracefully, rather than inferiorly. I am aggressive in my love toward people, spawned by a desire to be loved; this is the way God has created me. My aggressiveness causes some to misjudge me, causing them to avoid me. To be treated that way by those who call themselves Christian, cause me to question their Christianity, if they truly have Him in their heart. Unconditional love will always cause us to forgive without being asked, to not hold grudges, and to love people even if they are not worthy of it.

> **By this shall all men know that ye are my disciples, if ye have love one to another."**
> **John 13:35**

Jesus said in the gospel of John, "If God where your father you would love me". Jesus wept over Jerusalem because they rejected him, he did not weep for himself but for them, because of the judgment of God that was to come upon them having rejected Him. God is longsuffering toward man, desiring their salvation, but if we reject Him He will reject us, with no remorse. If we reject Him too many times He will eventually give us over to a reprobate mind, a conscience void of conviction, no longer to approach us again. **When we follow God, Jesus, and the Holy Spirit's approach toward rejection, the "Enemy" will not be able to afflict our soul when we are rejected.**

In the gospel of John when Jesus said, "if God were your father you would love me," He was saying, if you were living your life to please God He would be your Father, you would love me, but because you are living your life to please yourself and others you are of your father the devil. The Religious live their lives to please themselves and others. When they encounter someone who is living their life to please God, they reject and despise them, just as the religious leaders did to Jesus, to the point of crucifying him.

The Lord has shown me that if I am living my life to please Him and not man, the bite of rejection cannot hurt me. It is when I am trying to win the approval of others (a popularity contest), that approach causes me to be wounded, and to suffer depression when I am rejected. For a Christian to suffer from the effects of rejection it is not a mental or emotional problem that a pill can remedy, that is for a person who is not a Christian.

When it is a Christian who suffers with rejection it is a spiritual problem that only living our life to please God, not man, can remedy. When you are confronted with rejection focus your attention on God and who He has called you to be, rather than on the one who is rejecting you. It is what He thinks of you that matters most, not what others think of you. In the end of days it will not be them who will be your Judge.

When we are seeking to be <u>popular with God</u>, and are rejected by someone, we will not weep for ourselves, but for the one who is rejecting us. That is what Jesus did over Jerusalem (Luke 19:41-44) because of the judgment of God that was going to hit them for rejecting Him. I have been astonished to find that the very ones who we think are "popular", suffer with rejection. No one is exempt, but not everyone handles it the same way. Unconditional love (charity, 1 Cor. 13), will cause me not to reject anyone, or at less try not to make them feel rejected. I say, "try not to", because many things we do and say are perceived to be different than we intend, while harmless in the intent, not everyone interprets what we say or do the same as we intended the action. Once again, if I am living my life to please and be popular with God, the bite of rejection from others will not hurt me.

CHAPTER 9
~ THE NICOLAITANS ~

Easton's Bible Dictionary

The church at Ephesus (Revelation 2:6 </OnlineStudyBible/bible. cgi?passage=re+2:6>) is commended for hating the "deeds" of the Nicolaitans, and the church of Pergamos is blamed for having them who hold their "doctrines" (15). They were seemingly a class of professing Christians, who sought to introduce into the church a false freedom or licentiousness, thus abusing Paul's doctrine of grace (Compare 2 Peter 2:15,16,19 </OnlineStudyBible/bible.cgi? Passage=2pe+2:15,16,19>) , and were probably identical with those who having a false freedom held the doctrine of Baalam (q.v.), Revelation 2:14 </OnlineStudyBible/ bible.cgi? Passage=re+2:14>. Licentiousness definition: **Main Entry: li·cen·tious Pronunciation:** lī-'sen(t)-sh&s **Function:** *adjective* **Etymology:** Latin *licentiosus,* from *licentia* 1: lacking legal or moral restraints; *especially*: disregarding sexual restraints. **2:** marked by disregard for strict rules of correctness, **(disregard for holy living)**

Robertson's Word Pictures of the New Testament

So thou also (outwß kai su). Thou and the church at Pergamum as Israel had the wiles of Balaam. **The teaching of the Nicolaitans likewise (thn didachn twn Nikolaitwn omoiwß).** See on 1 Corinthians 1:6 </ OnlineStudyBible/bible.cgi? Passage=1Co+1:6> for the Nicolaitans. The use of **omoiwß** (likewise) here shows that they followed Balaam in not obeying the decision of the Conference at Jerusalem (Acts 15:20,29

</OnlineStudyBible/bible.cgi? Passage=Ac+15:20,29>) about idolatry and fornication, with the result that they encouraged a return to pagan laxity of morals (Swete). Some wrongly hold that these Nicolaitans were Pauline Christians in the face of Colossians 3:5-8 </OnlineStudyBible/ bible.cgi? Passage=Col+3:5-8>; Ephesians 5:3-6 </OnlineStudyBible/ bible.cgi? Passage=Eph+5:3-6>

Smith's Bible Dictionary

(*Followers of Nicolas*), a sect mentioned in (Revelation 2:6,15) whose deeds was strongly condemned. They may have been identical with those who held the doctrine of Balaam. They seem to have held that it was lawful to eat things sacrificed to idols, and to commit fornication, in opposition to the decree of the Church rendered in (Acts 15:20,29) The teachers of the Church branded them with a name, which expressed their true character. The men who did and taught such things were followers of Balaam. (2 Peter 2:15; Jude 1:11) They, like the false prophet of Pethor, united brave words with evil deeds. In a time of persecution, when the eating or not eating of things sacrificed to idols was more than ever a crucial test of faithfulness, they persuaded men more than ever that was a thing indifferent. (Revelation 2:13,14) This was bad enough, but there was a yet worse evil.

Mingling themselves in the orgies of idolatrous feasts, they brought the impurities of those feasts into the meetings of the Christian Church. And all this was done, it must be remembered not simply as an indulgence of appetite: but as a part of a system, supported by a "doctrine," accompanied by the boast of a prophetic illumination, (2 Peter 2:1) It confirms the view which has been taken of their character to find that stress is laid in the first instance on the "deeds" of the Nicolaitans. To hate those deeds is a sign of life in a Church that otherwise is weak and faithless. (Revelation 2:6) To tolerate them is well nigh to forfeit the glory of having been faithful under persecution. (Revelation 2:14,15)

CHAPTER 10
- THYATIRA -

And unto the angel of the church in Thyatira write; These things saith the Son of God, who hath his eyes like unto a flame of fire, and his feet are like fine brass; I know thy works, and charity, and service, and faith, and thy patience, and thy works; and the last to be more than the first. Notwithstanding I have a few things against thee, because thou sufferest that woman Jezebel, which calleth herself a prophetess, to teach and to seduce my servants to commit fornication, and to eat things sacrificed unto idols. And I gave her space to repent of her fornication; and she repented not. Behold, I will cast her into a bed, and them that commit adultery with her into great tribulation, except they repent of their deeds. And I will kill her children with death; and all the churches shall know that I am he which searcheth the reins and hearts: and I will give unto every one of you according to your works. But unto you I say, and unto the rest in Thyatira, as many as have not this doctrine, and which have not known the depths of Satan, as they speak; I will put upon you none other burden. But that which ye have already hold fast till I come. And he that overcometh, and keepeth my works unto the end, to him will I give power over the nations: And he shall rule them with a rod of iron; as the vessels of a potter shall they be broken to shivers: even as I received of my Father. And I will give him

the morning star. He that hath an ear, let him hear what the
Spirit saith unto the churches.
Revelation 2:18-29

Revelation 2:18

And unto the angel [Pastor] of the church in **Thyatira** [odor of
affliction] write

[This city was a military city, where purple clothing was made,
and other crafts flourished, Lydia in the book of Acts was from
this city, Acts 16:14.]

These things **saith the Son of God**, [second in command, Jesus
signifies it is him speaking, this is significant to me for Jesus
emphasized his status, or position in the Godhead]

who hath his **eyes** like unto a flame of fire, [a consuming fire,
Hebrews 12:29, for judgment] and his **feet** are like fine brass;
[feet to crush, for judgment]

2:19

I know thy **works**, [Gk: deeds]

and **charity**, (Gk: unconditional love)

and **service**, [Gk: Christian service, church offices, pastor,
evangelist, etc.]

and **faith**, [Gk: steadfast, unwavering faith]

and thy **patience**, [Gk: perseverance]

and thy **works**; [Gk: acts, deeds]

and **the last to be more than the first.** [Obvious growth, and
improvement]

2:20 **the deeds of Jezebel and the judgment of God against her sin,
v. 20-23**

Notwithstanding I have a few things against thee, because thou sufferest that woman Jezebel, which calleth herself a prophetess, to teach and to seduce my servants <u>to commit fornication</u>, [sexual immorality] and <u>to eat things sacrificed unto idols</u>. *(Baal, or type of idol worship)

[Another name for Jezebel is Sambatha or Sembathe; she was a female sorcerer, fortuneteller.] [There was a temple to this type of cult.] [The name Jezebel could be a symbolic name to describe the type of spirit that controlled her.]

2:21

And I gave her space to repent of her **fornication**; [Gk: all forms of sexual immorality and abominations] and she repented not.

2:22 **Jezebel and those who follow her will be judged**

Behold, I will cast her into a **bed,** [a bed of judgment]

and them that commit adultery with her into **great tribulation,** [Gk: judgment, tribulation, affliction, trouble, anguish, persecution, burdened, and to be afflicted] except they repent of their deeds.

2:23

And I will kill her children [followers, disciples] with **death;** [Gk: implies physical death with the judgment of hell, and spiritual death while living]

and all the churches shall know that <u>I am he which searcheth the reins and hearts</u>: [Nothing is a secret from God. They have a spiritual heart problem, not necessarily so obvious to those who see them, but God knew their heart; Psalms 7:9, Jeremiah 17:10]

and I will give unto every one of you according to your **works.** [Gk: blessing or cursing according to whether it is righteous living or sinful]

[WORKS: obedience or disobedience, Gk: conduct, lifestyle, acts, deeds, labor, doings]

2:24

But unto you I say, and unto the rest in Thyatira, as many as have not this doctrine, and which have not known the depths of Satan, as they speak; I will put upon you none other **burden.** [Gk: the persecution, and trouble they suffer][No judgment of God against them]

2:25

But that which ye have already **hold fast** till I come. [Be steadfast and unmovable]

2:26

And he that overcometh, and **keepeth my works** unto the end,

[Jesus' works was to do only what God told him to do, obedience. A command has been given to us to follow in the steps of Him who never sinned/disobeyed (*1 Peter 2:21*)]

to him will I give power over the nations: [the meek (*obedient*) shall inherit the earth, (*Matthew 5:5*)]

2:27

And **he shall rule them with a rod of iron;** [he shall have great authority, boldness, anointing] as the vessels of a potter shall they [the nations] be broken to shivers: even as I received of my Father.

2:28

And I will give him the morning star. [Jesus will give of himself to us, a place of fellowship with him, dwelling, and oneness]

2:29

He that hath an ear [heart understanding, Holy Spirit revelation] let him hear what the Spirit saith unto the **churches** (plural). [What the Spirit says to his people.]

Thyatira was a northern city of Asia Minor, used as one of Rome's garrison cities against attacks in that region of the country, thus there was a military presence. It was a city where many businesses flourished, a few of which wherein purple dye and clothing was manufactured. Lydia, mentioned in Acts 16:14, was a part of this craft. **The population understood military rule and authority.** It was with this fact that Jesus describes himself: **These things saith the Son of God, who hath his eyes like unto a flame of fire, and his feet are like fine brass.** I am in awe, it was as if Jesus was saying to the church, I am head commander of God's army with the power to win every battle, repent or suffer the consequences of your rebellion! (Revelation 19:11-16)

As with all of the churches the Lord commends the Saints of Thyatira for what faithfulness to the doctrine of Christ they adhered to, yet there is fault to be reckoned with, similar to that of Pergamos. The last statement in v.19, "**and thy works** (acts, deeds) **and the last to be more than the first**", shows the church's humanitarian deeds were on the increase, but their ability to discern a demonic present in their midst had fallen behind. Just as with Ephesus, intimacy with God was a declining factor.

Jezebel, the name being believed to be symbolic of the demonic spirit that controlled her rather than her actual name, had a place of authority in the church. The history of this time gives her actual name as either Sambatha or Sembathe who practiced sorceries and fortune telling, she is believed to have been the lead practitioner and sibyl of the temple erected to fortune telling, known for her prophetic utterances which were actually demonic in nature and not from God as some would have believed. Her abilities were similar to that of Simon the sorcerer mentioned in Acts 8:9-24, and Elymas (Acts 13:6-11). Jezebel of the Old Testament was a very evil woman for whom the death of many of the prophets (preachers of the word) was accredited to [1 Kings 18:4]. Just as did Simon, Sambatha (Jezebel) had an acute ability to deceive the church in believing she was a prophet of God, when in reality she was a devil in sheep's clothing.

It would appear to me that just as with Simon, Sambatha believed the message of salvation, what Jesus did to satisfy God's requirement for our atonement, for our sins to be forgiven and the promise of eternal life to be granted. Simon and Sambatha's faith in the message was not the transforming faith (so it would appear) that causes souls to receive God's righteous nature, and the sinful nature to be cast off. Their initial act of repentance, going through the motions as a ritualistic act rather than a changed heart, was convincing enough to deceive the Christians to believe they had truly received the born again experience associated with true and sincere repentance from sin, when in reality they had not. In process of time Simon had been exposed for his lack of sincere faith (as stated in Acts 8:20-23), but Sambatha had yet to be exposed as only having a religious experience with Christ instead of a life altering one.

Sambatha had a prophetic ability v.20, like that of Balaam (The story of Balaam is found in Numbers 22:5 thru 31:16). Although Balaam was able to be used by God to bless the children of Israel, his heart was that of a diviner (Numbers 22:7) and an enchanter (Numbers 24:1) following his own desires and greed (Jude 1:11), which eventually got him killed along with those who wanted the children of Israel to be cursed (Numbers 31:8). Sambatha had a much greater foothold for Satan v.24 in the church of Thyatira, than the instructors of the doctrines of Balaam and of the Nicoliatans did in the church of Pergamos. For, God did not say that these instructors had a position of ministry in the church at Pergamos, Sambatha had a position of ministry at Thyatira.

If Sambatha had truly repented of her sins out of a sincere heart of truth, she apparently was not totally willing to give up on her temple practices and beliefs. She obviously had a gift for teaching, possibly to be a fast learner concerning the doctrine of Christ, yet was mixing her idol worship and sexually immoral doctrine with the doctrine of Christ, being subtle enough not to be stopped by the Pastor who himself may not have been as faithful a testimony for Christ as he ought to have been. Whatever the reason Sambatha was allowed to continue as a teacher in the church.

In v.21 God was being longsuffering toward Sambatha. God having mercy on her would seem to imply that she did have some sort of respect for the things of God, but not enough to repent of what she was doing. Since she would not repent God's judgment v.22-23 was going to be laid against her, and those who chose to be a part of what she was teaching and doing. It is this same attitude that God has toward those who are Lukewarm, giving them a space of time to repent.

The Lord is not slack concerning his promise, as some men count slackness; but is longsuffering to us-ward, not willing that any should perish, but that all should come to

repentance. And account that the longsuffering of our Lord
is salvation;...

2 Peter 3:9, 15a

God's final words to Thyatira, was to pronounce blessing on those
who were being faithful to the doctrine of Christ and <u>actively complying
with His perfect will for their life</u> to "**keep my works**". He promises
power over the nations and His favor to be upon them not only now, but
forever. The works of Jesus was to obey all that the Father told Him to
do (John 8:28-29), and so is it for those who are the true Saints of God.
It is the Saints who will reign with Jesus during the Millennium (Rev.
20:4-5).

**Blessed are the poor in spirit, For theirs is the kingdom
of heaven. Blessed are those who mourn, For they shall be
comforted. <u>Blessed are the meek</u> (*obedient*)<u>, For they shall
inherit the earth</u>. Blessed are those who hunger and thirst
for righteousness, For they shall be filled. Blessed are the
merciful, For they shall obtain mercy. Blessed are the pure in
heart, For they shall see God. Blessed are the peacemakers,
For they shall be called sons of God. Blessed are those who are
persecuted for righteousness' sake, For theirs is the kingdom
of heaven. Blessed are you when they revile and persecute
you, and say all kinds of evil against you falsely for my sake.
Rejoice and be exceedingly glad, for great is your reward in
heaven...**

Matthew 5:3-12a

And I saw thrones, and they sat upon them, and judgment
was given unto them: and I saw the souls of them that were
beheaded for the witness of Jesus, and for the word of God,
and which had not worshipped the beast, neither his image,
neither had received his mark upon their foreheads, or in their
hands; and they lived and reigned with Christ a thousand
years. But the rest of the dead lived not again until the
thousand years were finished. This is the first resurrection.

Revelation 20:4-5

The name Thyatira means "odor of affliction." In v.23 the Lord makes something else clear about Himself, **"and all the churches shall know that I am he which searcheth the reins and hearts:"** Whatever the significant reason for Thyatira being named, being a city occupied by the Roman military caused the population to know mental and emotional affliction even to the depths of their soul and spirit. The people of the city were prime for the gospel of Jesus Christ.

> **Oh let the wickedness of the wicked come to an end; but establish the just: for the righteous God trieth the hearts and reins.**
>
> **Psalms 7:9**

> **I the LORD search the heart, I try the reins, even to give every man according to his ways, and according to the fruit of his doings.**
>
> **Jeremiah 17:10**

As Christians, those of us who are a threat to the kingdom of darkness by virtue of our having the righteous nature of God in us (being born-again), and even the more so those of us who are filled with His power and the gifts of the Holy Spirit (the greater anointing), we know what it is to be afflicted by those who dwell in the darkness, whether it is human or demon. <u>For, we are not of this world any longer although we are in it.</u> God's favor is on those who call themselves "Christian" obeying, yielding to His perfect will, but his wrath is on those who are Religious, Hypocrite, and Lukewarm.

God is being longsuffering and merciful attempting to draw them to repentance. God is calling to those of us who call ourselves "Christian," having some level of respect for the things of God, but not willing to totally repent of worldliness and carnal pursuits that bring dishonor and contempt on Him in the sight of those who do not know Him as <u>Lord</u> and Savoir, to **REPENT** v.21. We can not live our life like that of Jezebel, doing the things of the occult, horoscopes, fortune telling, and the like, then expect God to grant us eternal life, He will not. Instead of favor His judgment will be upon us. This is especially true for those who have a place of ministry in the church, whatever is that position. For there are those who "idolize" ministry, and will be swayed to follow the example they see in us, whether it be poor or rich in total surrender to the perfect will of God.

For the name of God is blasphemed among the Gentiles through you, as it is written.
Romans 2:24

I have given them thy word; and the world hath hated them, because they are not of the world, even as I am not of the world. I pray not that thou shouldest take them out of the world, but that thou shouldest keep them from the evil. They are not of the world, even as I am not of the world.
John 17:14-16

The majority of the Believers, not the Saints, at Thyatira had become comfortable with living the life style of the surrounding community. Satan found a helper in Sambatha who had the "demon of Jezebel, a killer of the prophets" in her, to cause those who had a willing heart to live according to a "relaxed moral code" rather than God's "standard of holiness," so that their names would be <u>blotted out of the book of life.</u> We must be vigilant not to allow the sinful nature that is in our flesh, and any outside stimuli which call to us from unconverted souls and demonic forces, cause us to sleep, slumber, and walk in deadness of spirit (as do foolish virgins), otherwise the wrath of God will be against us. If sincerely having given our heart to Christ, which would be the cause of our living in the Spirit, then let us also walk in the Spirit. **Obey Him**, for in doing so the favor of God will be on us.

If ye love me, keep my commandments. He that hath my <u>commandments, and keepeth them, he it is that loveth me: and he that loveth me shall be loved of my Father, and I will love him,</u> and will manifest myself to him Jesus answered and said unto him, If a man love me, he will keep my words: and my Father will love him, and we will come unto him, and make our abode with him.
John 14:15, 21, 23

For this is the love of God, that we keep his commandments: and his commandments are not grievous.

1 John 5:3

There is therefore now no condemnation to them which are in Christ Jesus, who walk not after the flesh, but after the Spirit.

Romans 8:1

That the righteousness of the law might be fulfilled in us, who walk not after the flesh, but after the Spirit.

Romans 8:4

This I say then, Walk in the Spirit, and ye shall not fulfil the lust *(desires)* of the flesh.

Galatians 5:16

If we live in the Spirit, let us also walk in the Spirit.

Galatians 5:25

CHAPTER 11
- S A R D I S -

And unto the angel of the church in Sardis write; These things saith he that hath the seven Spirits of God, and the seven stars; I know thy works, that thou hast a name that thou livest, and art dead. Be watchful, and strengthen the things which remain, that are ready to die: for I have not found thy works perfect before God. Remember therefore how thou hast received and heard, and hold fast, and repent. If therefore thou shalt not watch, I will come on thee as a thief, and thou shalt not know what hour I will come upon thee. Thou hast a few names even in Sardis which have not defiled their garments; and they shall walk with me in white: for they are worthy. He that overcometh, the same shall be clothed in white raiment; and I will not blot out his name out of the book of life, but I will confess his name before my Father, and before his angels. He that hath an ear, let him hear what the Spirit saith unto the churches.

Revelation 3:1-6

Revelation 3:1

And unto the angel of the church in **Sardis** [prince of joy] write;

These things saith he that hath the **seven Spirits of God**, (see chap. 1:4, 4:5) ["Seven Spirits" could be a description of His personality and character] [Sevenfold Spirit, or the fullness of the Godhead dwelling in Him bodily] [7 horns and 7 eyes = seven Spirits of God, chap. 5:6]

and **the seven stars**; [Pastors]

I know thy **works**, [Gk: acts, deeds]

that thou hast a name that thou **livest, and art dead**. [Only have a religious experience]

3:2

Be watchful, [Gk: vigilant, Jesus said watch, Matthew 24:42] and strengthen (*steadfast, unmovable*) the things which remain, [repent of lack of commitment]

that are ready to die: for I have not found thy works **perfect** (*acceptable, GK: complete*) before God. [You are not doing God's perfect will, falling short of His standard of holiness]

3:3

Remember therefore how thou hast received and heard, and hold fast, and repent. [*You are not ready for me nor able to know when I am coming, foolish virgins*]

If therefore thou shalt not watch, [if you will not be vigilant; what I say to you I say to all watch, Mark 13:37]

I will come on thee as a thief, [unexpected: 1 Thess.5: 1-10, and Rev 16:14]

and thou shalt not know what hour <u>I will come upon thee</u>. [Swooping down on, attack]

3:4

Thou hast a few names even in Sardis which have not defiled their garments; [*who do not live worldly lives*] and they shall <u>walk with me in white</u>: [white: a sign of righteousness, purity, holy living. Walk with me: fellowship]

for they are **worthy**. [Repentance, and obedience to God's perfect will make us worthy] [Pray to be accounted worthy, Luke 21:36]

3:5

He that <u>overcometh,</u> [endures to the end, receiving the end of our faith the salvation of our soul, 1 Peter 1:9]

the same shall **be clothed in white raiment; and I will not blot out his name out of the book of life,** [1 old testament ref, 2 in Rev][Ex. 32:32, those who commit habitual sin against me I will blot out]

but I will confess his name before my Father, and before his angels. [Ashamed not ashamed, Mark 8:38]

3:6

He that hath an ear, **let him hear what the Spirit saith** unto the churches (plural).

[Let him understand what the Spirit is revealing, showing to the churches, the individual Christian; a hidden meaning]

Sardis means "Prince of Joy", but we can see from God's description of the church, that the church is far from it. Not only had the joy of the Lord (".... For the joy of the Lord is your strength." Nehemiah 8:10) departed from their life, so did the Holy Spirit and the ability to discern that He had (liken unto that of Samson, Judges 16:20). **The church had deceived them self in believing that all is well in their relationship with God.** When we choose to walk in worldliness and carnal pleasure, after having sincerely given our heart to Christ, not only will God's presence not be with us, neither will His joy. Here is how God's joy was with Jesus and how His joy will be with us. When we live our life as Jesus did, <u>in full obedience to the perfect will of God</u>, the same abundant joy that Jesus had will be ours also.

Thou hast loved righteousness, and hated iniquity; therefore God, even thy God, hath anointed thee with the oil of gladness above thy fellows.

Hebrews 1:9

The distinction spoken of in v.1 "the seven Spirits of God," has to do with Jesus having the all-encompassing fullness of God's Spirit within Him. Another interpretation of this is that this is referring to the personality and character of God. With this second interpretation, Revelation 5:6 could imply that God's personality and character can be found in every cell and atom of creation. What ever the exact meaning Jesus is describing Himself this way to Sardis, and it is likely that they understood the meaning.

John to the seven churches which are in Asia: Grace be unto you, and peace, from him which is, and which was, and which is to come; and from the seven Spirits which are before his throne;

Revelation 1:4

And out of the throne proceeded lightnings and thunderings and voices: and there were seven lamps of fire burning before the throne, which are the seven Spirits of God.

Revelation 4:5

And I beheld, and, lo, in the midst of the throne and of the four beasts, and in the midst of the elders, stood a Lamb as it had been slain, having seven horns and seven eyes, which are the seven Spirits of God sent forth into all the earth.

Revelation 5:6

For it pleased the Father that in him should <u>all fullness dwell</u>:

Colossians 1:19

Beware lest any man spoil you through philosophy and vain deceit, after the tradition of men, after the rudiments of the world, and not after Christ. For in him dwelleth all the

fullness of the Godhead bodily. And ye are complete in him, which is the head of all principality and power:
Colossians 2:8-10

For the invisible things of him from the creation of the world are clearly seen, being understood by the things that are made, even his eternal power and Godhead; so that they are without excuse:
Romans 1:20

Like many churches today the church of Sardis had become a "country club" type of church. Church where, for the most part, no one was being won to Christ, and the attitude in their gathering together was more for socializing than for prayer and to worship God out of a sincere heart of truth and devotion to Him. Most likely, because they were "**dead**" spiritually v.1, persecution of the church was not like that of the other cities, if it existed at all.

Sardis, unlike the humanitarian deeds of Thyatira, and the passion of Ephesus to fulfill the Great Commission to win the population of Ephesus to Christ, had just about if not altogether given up on doing anything for the kingdom of God, whether it be the spiritual growth of the "Christians", or winning Sardis to Christ. There obviously was some kind of maintenance of the church going on, if not by the Pastor, at least by those in the church who did have a passion for Christ on a personal level. In v.4 the Lord said, "**Thou hast a <u>few names</u> even in Sardis which have not defiled their garments.**" It was because of the few saints who were "working out their own salvation with fear and trembling (Phil. 2:12)" praying for revival in Sardis, that God was speaking to the church.

The Lord covers numerous specifics about this church, which is a declaration of what God requires of us, for us to be assured the salvation of our soul and what is a favorable or unfavorable attitude of God toward those who profess to be His people. God says in verse 1 "**I know thy works** [*Gk, acts, deeds*]**, that thou hast a name that thou livest, and art dead.**" The Church had become <u>**complacent**</u> (self-satisfied and unconcerned), causing the church to be like the pagan temples around it, just another place for religious expression. This attitude was causing the gospel of Christ to become just a philosophy for moral living in the midst of a pagan belief system, rather than a radically changed spiritual nature, from that of a Sinner to a Saint.

In verse 2-3, "**Be watchful, and strengthen the things which remain, that are ready to die: for I have not found thy works perfect before God. Remember therefore how thou hast received and heard, and hold fast, and repent...**" God's command to the believers in Sardis is to become vigilant, repent of being self-satisfied, content, and unconcerned, or I will bring swift judgment upon you. The majority of the Believers in Sardis had become what God calls <u>cold</u>, neither lukewarm nor hot. Their walk with him had become unacceptable, "**I have not found thy works perfect before God.**"

> **Watch therefore: for ye know not what hour your Lord doth come.**
> **Matthew 24:42**

> **Watch therefore, for ye know neither the day nor the hour wherein the Son of man cometh.**
> **Matthew 25:13**

> **Watch ye therefore: for ye know not when the master of the house cometh, at even, or at midnight, or at the cockcrowing, or in the morning: Lest coming suddenly he find you sleeping. And what I say unto you I say unto all, Watch.**
> **Mark 13:35-37**

Although these scriptures speak of Jesus' return for His church, the attitude of God is no different concerning discipline. As in Revelation 3:2 the same Greek word translated "watchful" and those in Matthew and Mark translated "watch" is used, thus **Jesus' exhortation is in reference to <u>vigilance</u>. We are to build upon, and fortify our resolve to obey God's perfect will for our life, TO LIVE IT.** If we choose not to correct ourselves, God will do it when we least expect it, v3. This attitude of God is the same if we are not being vigilant to maintain a deep intimate relationship with Him, when He comes for His Saints we will be left behind *(foolish virgins).

But that which beareth thorns and briers is rejected, and is nigh unto cursing; whose end is to be burned.

Hebrews 6:8

We are not to allow the seeming delay of Jesus' return to cause us to become complacent in our walk with Christ, as we grow older in Him. Our walk with the Lord should become much deeper, more intimate with each passing day. We are to become more passionate, and hungry to be used by Him to be a manifestation of His glory, power, and abundant life that only He can give, even in our "golden years." Our age is not a barrier to God using us to effect change for His kingdom, to be used for why He created us, and let us continue to live. (Abraham and Sarah are good examples)

It is with this, as God said to Sardis, He says to us, who have forgotten, "<u>Remember</u> **therefore how thou hast received and heard, and hold fast, and repent.**" The Word of God declares it, and those who have revelation from God preach and write about it, TAKE HEED AND REPENT! I shared earlier "**God allows difficulties and bad experiences to happen to us to draw us closer to Him, not to cause us to abandon Him.**" <u>We learn obedience through the things we suffer</u> (temptation, trials, testing, and discipline). If we choose not to do something about this ourselves, then as a Father to a son or daughter, God will. God therefore says, **remember**. In verse 3 the Lord continues, "If therefore thou shalt not watch, I will come on thee as a thief (*unexpected*), and thou shalt not know what hour I will come upon thee."

And beside this, giving all diligence, add to your faith virtue; and to virtue knowledge; And to knowledge temperance; and to temperance patience; and to patience godliness; And to godliness brotherly kindness; and to brotherly kindness charity. For if these things be in you, and abound, they make you that ye shall neither be barren nor unfruitful in the knowledge of our Lord Jesus Christ. <u>But he that lacketh these things is blind</u>, and cannot see afar off, and <u>hath forgotten</u> that he was purged from his old sins.

2 Peter 1:5-9

Watch ye therefore, and <u>pray always, that ye may be accounted worthy</u> to escape all these things that shall come to pass, and to stand before the Son of man.

Luke 21:36

For as the body without the spirit is dead, so faith without works (*deeds, acts, labors*) **is dead also.**

James 2:26

It is true that we are saved by grace through faith and that there is nothing we can do, no good moral deed, nor anything that could merit salvation on our part. There is nothing that we can do that would cause God to pardon our sin and grant us access to eternal life, for the exception of repenting of our sin to accept God's gift of salvation, this God has established to be a fact. Good works do not save us, but holy living or more specifically, obedience to God's perfect will for our life, His every desire which He speaks to us being fulfilled, **after repentance**, guarantees the salvation of our soul through and by grace and faith when we pass from this life.

We must read and study God's word and be faithful to prayer daily, fasting, church attendance, and to fellowship (sharing what God reveals to us about His word and Himself) with one another. We are to be faithful to do what we can do without God's help, and trust Him to help us to do what we cannot do without His help. It is when we become <u>complacent</u>, <u>lack vigilance</u>, and <u>choose to forget </u>the exhortations of God's word, as well as not doing those necessary things that will strengthen our walk with God, those things that will cause intimate fellowship with Him, that will cause use to fall under His WRATH instead of His FAVOR.

This is God's promise to those who comply with all of His expectations, **who choose to obey His perfect will:** verse 4, **"Thou hast a few names even in Sardis which have not defiled their garments; and they shall walk with me in white: for they are worthy.** To defile our garments is to become like the Believers, not Saints, at Sardis became, self-satisfied and unconcerned. Faith alone does not save us; it is by grace through faith and obedience, complying with what the grace of God teaches us.

For the grace of God that bringeth salvation hath appeared to all men, Teaching us that, denying ungodliness and worldly

lusts, we should live soberly, righteously, and godly, in this present world; Looking for that blessed hope, and the glorious appearing of the great God and our Saviour Jesus Christ;

Titus 2:11-13

Do we then make void the law through faith? God forbid: yea, we establish the law.

Romans 3:31

Behold, I come as a thief. Blessed is he that watcheth, and keepeth his garments, lest he walk naked, and they see his shame.

Revelation 16:15

Follow peace with all men, and holiness, without which no man shall see the Lord:

Hebrews 12:14

(holiness: Gk. consecration, purification, the effect of consecration, sanctification of heart and life)

God's final word to Sardis and His word to us is this: "**He that overcometh, the same shall be clothed in white raiment; and <u>I will not blot out his name out of the book of life</u>, but I will confess his name before my Father, and before his angels. He that hath an ear, let him hear what the Spirit saith unto the churches, v.5.**

In the first few days or weeks of my conversion, I was praying to the Lord about some Christians I had already become familiar with. I do not remember my exact words, but in praying for them I was concerned about their eternal end, if they would be His when they died. God gave me a sure word about some but not everyone. Those who He did not give me a sure word about caused me to cry.

While praying with crying for them, I heard what I thought was someone else crying also. I stopped to listen, but so did the other crying. If I remember correctly, I started praying and crying again, hearing the other crying too. Then I asked, Lord why are you crying? He said, because you are.

More than thirty years later I still remember His word to me. When having given some thought to Rev 3:5, I remembered the sure word

God gave to me about the ones who would be with Him forever and the promise He made to the Saints in Sardis (those who had not defiled their garments), a word that He makes to those of us today who obey Him as they did. **You will be clothed in white and I will not blot out your name out of my book.**

When we become <u>complacent</u> in our walk with Christ, the sinful nature bound in our flesh, will get a foothold against the testimony of Jesus in our life. <u>**Through the mercy and longsuffering of God, the Holy Spirit will continue to work with us to seek to improve our relationship with Him**</u>. The Enemy of our soul, in the interim, will have been given the liberty to make us ashamed of the gospel of Christ. It is with this, that we will not do the "work of an evangelist" (2 Timothy 4:5).

When the occasion arises, to glorify God in the hearing of another person, we will shun doing it. Guilt over our lack of total surrender to God's perfect will for our life will be the reason for some of us, while for others, it will be out of a blatant disregard for the things of God, fueled out of having fallen into a religious experience concerning the things of God. The second reason is what happened to those in the church of Sardis. Here is what Jesus says about this issue:

> **Also I say unto you, Whosoever shall confess me before men, him shall the Son of man also confess before the angels of God: But he that denieth me before men shall be denied before the angels of God.**
> **Luke 12:8-9**

The promise of Jesus, "**I will not blot out his name out of the book of life, but I will confess his name before my Father, and before his angels**" is to those of us who "**have not defiled their garments.**" Being vigilant, aggressively cultivating a deep intimate love affair with God our Father, and obeying Him, will not only by our changed life be a testimony for Him, but also by the words that come out of our mouth.

> **Let no corrupt communication proceed out of your mouth, but that which is good to the use of edifying, that it may minister grace unto the hearers.**
> **Ephesians 4:29**

CHAPTER 12
~ THE LAW OF CHRIST ~

Bear ye one another's burdens, and so fulfill the law of Christ.

Galatians 6:2

To them that are without law, as without law, (being not without law to God, but under the law to Christ,) that I might gain them that are without law.

1 Corinthians 9:21

There is a law of Christ; the greatest aspect of this law is LOVE. Love and devotion to God is to be paramount in our walk with Him, which would flow toward others. Another aspect of the law is Obedience to God and to Christ; it is not a grievous command when spawned out of love for Him. There is a love that exceeds our own, not just for Him but for others also. **It is the <u>hereditary element</u> of His Love that flows out of the <u>righteous nature of God</u> that is in our inner man, our spirit.**

"Bear ye one another's burdens", burden takes on many characteristics. These characteristics being: heaviness, weight, burden, trouble, tribulation, and persecution. The form of love that is compassion compels us to help one another through emotional and physical trauma, and not to add to the "burden" what ever form it takes.

For this is the love of God, that we keep his commandments: and his commandments are not grievous.

1 John 5:3

Greater love hath no man than this, that a man lay down his life for his friends.
John 15:13

And he answering said, Thou shalt love the Lord thy God with all thy heart, and with all thy soul, and with all thy strength, and with all thy mind; and thy neighbor as thyself.
Luke 10:27

If ye keep my commandments, ye shall abide in my love; even as I have kept my Father's commandments, and abide in his love.
John 15:10

If ye love me, keep my commandments.
John 14:15

Laying down our life for our friends, does not only cover dying in the place of someone else, but it is also the spiritual death to the sinful nature bound in our flesh, refusing to yield to its rebellious pull. Jesus is our example of death to self-will, self-desire, and self-ambition (1 Peter 2:21-22). It is because of His example that the Apostles did and taught the same. Death to self-will, self-desire, and self-ambition is a dying that others would live.

When we obey God with all of our heart, soul, strength, and mind this is how we show God's love to others. Death to the will of the sinful nature bound in our flesh, and obedience to God's perfect will is the ultimate testament to all people, (especially the "household of faith"), from which the glory of God and His love flows to the world. When we are in total obedience to Him, He promises to manifest the fullness of His Glory through our life to the world (Isaiah 58:6-14).

As we have therefore opportunity, let us do good unto all men, especially unto them who are of the household of faith.
Galatians 6:10

Then shall thy light break forth as the morning, and thine health shall spring forth speedily: and thy righteousness shall go before thee; the glory of the LORD shall be thy rereward.
Isaiah 58:8

How did Jesus purchase eternal life for us? He died for our offenses and was raised again for our justification (Romans 4:25). How will these sinners, who I have mentioned ever receive this same eternal life, we have received in Christ? We must learn how to die that they may live, and learn how to die for others to live.

Obedience to God is not a grievous duty, but rather a joyous labor; that is, if we truly love God, as so many of us readily say we do. Total obedience to our Father is not an obedience because of demand, but rather out of love and reverence for the One who loves us, died and rose again for us, now at the right hand of God making intercession for us, according to God's will, in our behalf. Definitely so, and **a true Saint of God obeys Him, not because we have to, but because we want to.** The joy that accompanies total obedience to our Father and Being One with Him, having true fellowship with our Creator, is beyond words to describe. This wonderful place of fellowship, and total obedience, is within the reach of every one of us, if only we will seek God for the revealing of how to attain to it, then receive it and run with it.

The whole duty of man is to obey God, to humble ourselves (as Jesus did, Phil. 2:8), **submitting, to walk in full obedience to our Father,** so to have fellowship in the light, as He is in the light, which the Lord desires for us. God's desire for our fellowship though, is not as great as His desire for our joy, which He intended us to continually experience, before we sinned in Adam. **One of the most obvious reasons, why our Father wants us to have a continual abundance of joy, and desires our uninterrupted fellowship, is LOVE.**

When we have an overwhelming love for someone we want to be with them our every waking moment, this is God's love for us and His desire to fellowship, spend meaningful and positive time with us. I know what it is to be despised, rejected, and afflicted, to be in want of my brothers and sisters love and fellowship, unconditional acceptance by all, **like God is wanting ours,** to only be ignored or snubbed by the very ones who are supposed to love unconditionally, without partiality or bias.

The word of God says, "How can you love God if you don't love your brother" (I John 4:20)? By this shall all men know that you are my disciples if you love one another...John 13:35. Love covers the multitude of sins (fault) I Peter 4:8. In 2 Peter 1:5-7 the last virtue for true maturity in Christ is charity (**unconditional love**), something that many in the Church have very little of because of *the* constant practice of prejudice, or fault finding, *that stems from the sinful nature that is in the flesh*. Unconditional love resists prejudice and the tendency to find fault.

The law of Christ compels us to die to self-will, self-desire, and self-ambition, to be the example of Christ to the world, so that when they see us they see the Father, the Son, and the Holy Spirit. When Philip asked to see the Father, Jesus said that when seeing Him he was seeing the Father. In our daily routine of life, in whatever environment we find ourselves, when there is occasion to mingle was Sinners, the law of Christ which is not only love, but obedience to God and to Christ, will give us a boundary we are not to cross, a threshold concerning our association with them. A threshold and a boundary we are not to cross, concerning our conduct, behavior, and speech. This is what Paul was referring to when he spoke of being among those who were without the law; he was still bound by the law of Christ, as are we.

Philip saith unto him, Lord, shew us the Father, and it sufficeth us. Jesus saith unto him, Have I been so long time with you, and yet hast thou not known me, Philip? he that hath seen me hath seen the Father; and how sayest thou then, Shew us the Father?

John 14:8-9

Chapter 13
-PHILADELPHIA-

And to the angel of the church in Philadelphia write; These things saith he that is holy, he that is true, he that hath the key of David, he that openeth, and no man shutteth; and shutteth, and no man openeth; I know thy works: behold, I have set before thee an open door, and no man can shut it: for thou hast a little strength, and hast kept my word, and hast not denied my name. Behold, I will make them of the synagogue of Satan, which say they are Jews, and are not, but do lie; behold, I will make them to come and worship before thy feet, and to know that I have loved thee. Because thou hast kept the word of my patience, I also will keep thee from the hour of temptation, which shall come upon all the world, to try them that dwell upon the earth. Behold, I come quickly: hold that fast which thou hast, that no man take thy crown. Him that overcometh will I make a pillar in the temple of my God, and he shall go no more out: and I will write upon him the name of my God, and the name of the city of my God, which is new Jerusalem, which cometh down out of from my God: and I will write upon him my new name. He that hath an ear, let him hear what the Spirit saith unto the churches.
Revelation 3:7-13

Revelation 3:7

And to the angel (Pastor) of the church in **Philadelphia** [brotherly love] write;

These things saith he that is **holy**,

he that is **true**,

he that hath the **key of David**, [authority][God is saying all things are under His control] [The key of David: He has control of the key that opens, not only for a mission in the earth, but also to the temple of God where we will be pillars, v 12. (Pillar: a place of life eternal with God)]

he that **openeth**, and no man shutteth;

and **shutteth**, and no man openeth;

3:8

I know thy **works**: [Gk: acts, deeds, labor]

behold, **I have set before thee an open door, and no man can shut it:** [A door of <u>liberty</u> where oppression cannot stop us, <u>freedom</u> no one can take away, to do God's will]

for thou hast a **little strength**, [continue to persevere, strugglers make it, tenacity]

and hast **kept my word**, [have obeyed and held to true doctrine, uncompromising]

and hast **not denied my name**. [Have remained <u>faithful and true</u>]

3:9

Behold, I will make them of the **synagogue of Satan**, which say they are Jews, and are not, but do lie; (spiritual Jews, no circumcision of heart/ religious, hypocrite) behold, <u>I will make them to come and worship before thy feet,</u> (to be honored and respected) and <u>to know that I have loved thee.</u> (God will show who is accepted and who is not) Romans 9:22-26

3:10

Because thou hast kept <u>the word of **my patience**,</u> (Rev 13:7-10 & 14:9-12)

I also will keep thee from the hour of **temptation,** (judgment) [Gk: testing, trial, proving] [Not appointed unto wrath, 1 Thess. 5:9]

which shall come upon all the world, to try them that dwell upon the earth. [The judgment of God because of their sin, the plagues and disasters foretold in later chapters.1 Thessalonians 5:3]

3:11

Behold, I come quickly: [As a thief, suddenly, unexpected] hold that fast which thou hast, [be a faithful and true testimony] that no man take thy crown. [Eternal reward; victor's reward, be not partaker of other men's sin. 1 Tim 5:22]

3:12

Him that overcometh will I make a **pillar** in the temple of my God, [Pillar: figurative meaning - permanent, dwelling forever in the presence of God] and he shall go no more out: (will have a place of rest)

and I will write upon him the <u>name of my God,</u>

and the <u>name of the city of my God,</u>

which is new Jerusalem, (**city of peace**) [God's name, the city's name, and Jesus' new name]

which cometh down out of heaven from my God: and I will write upon him **my new name.** [? The name on His thigh…chap 19:12?]

3:13

He that hath an ear, let him hear what the Spirit saith unto the churches (plural). The law of Christ was found in the church of Philadelphia. Philadelphia means: <u>brotherly love</u>.

For both he that sanctifieth and they who are sanctified are all of one: for which cause he is not ashamed to call them brethren,

Hebrews 2:11

And if children, then heirs; heirs of God, and joint-heirs with Christ; if so be that we suffer with him, that we may be also glorified together.

Romans 8:17

A man that hath friends must shew himself friendly: and there is a friend that sticketh closer than a brother.

Proverbs 18:24

Ye are my friends, if ye do whatsoever I command you.

John 15:14

When the Holy Spirit inspired the Apostles to write to any Church, God being aware of any unique culture and circumstances surrounding any particular church wherever a letter was to be written, had them to write accordingly. This could mean writing the same thing using the vernacular, expression common to their culture, character, and personality. So it is with what God gave John to write to the seven churches of Asia. With every church, Jesus describes Himself in a specific way to get their attention, to impress upon them the attitude of God's heart toward them.

Just as with Smyrna, God did not have a significant reprimand for the Believers at Philadelphia, but instead there was a special attitude of love for these believers, even like that of brother to brother. It was because of this attitude that He gives them a challenge v.8, and a special promise to help them with it, **"...I have set before thee an open door, and no man can shut it."** God wants to use these Saints and those like them, to influence the world for Christ. They are the Strugglers, who against all odds stand faithful and true.

These Christians possessed a special quality about them that was not found in the other churches v.8, for the exception of those in the churches who did not compromise their faith, and devotion to Christ and His doctrine for the doctrines of devils. Thus, Jesus describes Himself as **"...he that is holy, he that is true."** Jesus is the faithful and true witness, a statement He makes of Himself to the church of Laodicea. This is Jesus' view of the Philadelphia Saints, holy and true.

God says to Philadelphia, **"...for thou hast a little strength, and hast kept my word, and hast not denied my name. Behold, I will make them of the synagogue of Satan, which say they are Jews, and are not, but do lie; behold, I will make them to come and worship before thy feet, and to know that I have loved thee."** v.8-9

In the beginning paragraphs of this book I wrote: "One constant in all of the seven churches of Asia Minor, is the false and true believers. Each church has the spectators and the participators. The spectators of God's perfect will create trouble; the doers of God's perfect will do not. It is because of the true believers, that God is sending a message that encompasses God's reward and judgment." What is common in all churches so it was in Philadelphia, there where those who were Religious, Hypocrite, and Lukewarm.

The Philadelphia Saints struggling to walk with God had a heart desire and tenacity to excel, which caused God's favor to be granted them, even though their level of obedience was in need of improvement. The Religious, Hypocrite, and Lukewarm were not making it easy on them, they had "a little strength", but enough not to be swayed by those who had <u>none</u>. Here God makes a promise that He will exalt them in the sight of those in the church who were opposing them, **"...I will make them to come and worship before thy feet, and to know that I have loved thee."** v.9.

When writing about the church of Smyrna I wrote:
"It seems that the number one goal of some Believers is to destroy the faithfulness and loyalty of those Saints who are not walking in the same worldly and carnal lifestyle as they are. Just as it was with the foolish virgins attempt against the wise virgins to try to get them to "fall" to their level of worldliness by asking for their oil."

"As the day of Jesus' coming and the unveiling of Antichrist draws near the chasm between the sincere and true Christian and those who are not, is growing wider, so that it is becoming more evident who is truthfully one of God's children, and who just have a religious intellectual experience concerning the salvation that is found in Christ."

It is this "religious intellectual experience" (*gnosticism*) that fits the following scripture reference. Although common in the churches of Asia Minor, the following verse is a prophecy for the end time.

Ever learning, and never able to come to the knowledge of the truth.

2 Timothy 3:7

In the Old Testament God gave the prophet Zechariah a prophetic word about the Jews. Without dispute this is a prophecy for the biological Jew, but the same attitude of God toward the spiritual Jew (Romans 2:29) is no different, as is His word to the Saints of Philadelphia, "**... to come and worship before thy feet, and to know that I have loved thee.**" The intent of God is to exalt them.

Thus saith the LORD of hosts; In those days it shall come to pass, that ten men shall take hold out of all languages of the nations, even shall take hold of the skirt of him that is a Jew, saying, We will go with you: for we have heard that God is with you.

Zechariah 8:23

Rev 3:10 appears more to be a word of prophecy for the end time Christians, the statement "**Because thou hast kept the <u>word of my patience,</u> I also will keep thee from the hour of temptation, which shall come upon <u>all the world,</u> to try them that dwell upon the earth.**" The following two verses of text describe the patience and faith of Jesus and of the Saints. Those Christians who were keeping their "garments" and "crown" in Asia Minor, and those Saints throughout the ages unto this day, in the midst of any adverse circumstance Satan and those influenced by him throw at them, held and do hold to the patience and faith of Jesus and of the Saints. Those who choose to follow after worldliness and carnal pursuits, the destructive pleasures of sin, than to obey God, will have the wrath of God against them instead of His favor.

And it was given unto him to make war with the saints, and to overcome them: and power was given him over all kindred, and tongues, and nations. And all that dwell upon the earth shall worship him, whose names are not written in the book of life of the Lamb slain from the foundation of the world. If any man have an ear, let him hear. **He that leadeth into captivity shall go into captivity; he that killeth with the sword must be killed with the sword. Here is the patience and the faith of the saints.**
Revelation 13:7-10

And the third angel followed them, saying with a loud voice. If any man worship the beast and his image, and receive his mark in his forehead, or in his hand, the same shall drink of the wine of the wrath of God, which is poured out without mixture into the cup of his indignation; and he shall be tormented with fire and brimstone in the presence of the holy angels, and in the presence of the Lamb: And the smoke of their torment ascendeth up for ever and ever: and they have no rest day nor night, who worship the beast and his image, and whosoever receiveth the mark of his name. **Here is the patience of the saints; here are they that keep the commandments of God (*obey*), and the faith of Jesus.**
Revelation 14:9-12

God's exhortation to the Struggler, **"Behold, I come quickly: hold that fast which thou hast, that no man take thy crown."** v.11. His promise to those of us who overcome is a reserved spot in the presence of God and the New Jerusalem (pillar), a place of rest (go no more out), and the signet (the name) of God, Jesus, and the New Jerusalem upon them, that we are His. v.12

Let us therefore fear, lest, a promise being left us of entering into his rest, any of you should seem to come short of it...For he that is entered into his rest, he also hath ceased from his

own works, as God did from his. Let us labour therefore to enter into that rest, lest any man fall after the same example of unbelief.
Hebrews 4:1,10-11

The place of rest **"...he shall go no more out:"**v.12, is not only a promise reserved for eternity, but it is also an experience of "rest" that those who obey God's perfect will have all of the time, thus the exhortation of Hebrews 4:11, "Let us labor therefore to enter in that rest." For even in adversity there is a peace, assurance, faith, and hope that prevails in our spirit that the world, and any demonic attack, cannot take from us, which is bound in the promises of God. For, our fellowship is with the Father, and with His Son Jesus Christ.

That which we have seen and heard declare we unto you, that ye also may have fellowship with us: and truly our fellowship is with the Father, and with his Son Jesus Christ.
1 John 1:3

The Lord when speaking to the Saints in the churches of Asia, which is also a statement to all Believers spanning the centuries to this day, speaks of our garment and crown, to hold fast and not to let them be taken. In Matthew 22:2-14 Jesus gives a parable that ends with a statement of serious consequence, **"Many are called, but few are chosen"**. This parable Jesus directed toward the Religious leaders (Matthew 21:42-46).

As we read Matthew 22:2-14, the parable encompasses more than the nation of Israel. The "bad and good", speaks of those who believe among the Jews and the Gentile nations. He is speaking to the Religious of His day as a man among men. The "CHOSEN", are those who keep their garment and crown. The "Friend", Jesus speaks of that did not have a wedding garment, are those who have forfeited their garment and crown. They forfeited eternal life, by not complying with the dictates of God's "perfect will", to pursue Him with "ALL OF THEIR HEART". Matthew 22:13 tells what is the judgment of God against those who do not comply, **"... take him away, and cast him into outer darkness; there shall be weeping and gnashing of teeth."** This judgment of God is against the Religious, the Hypocrite, and the Lukewarm.

And if the righteous scarcely be saved, where shall the ungodly
and the sinner appear?

1 Peter 4:18

The kingdom of heaven is like unto a certain king, which made
a marriage for his son, And sent forth his servants to call
them that were bidden to the wedding: and they would not
come. Again, he sent forth other servants, saying, Tell them
which are bidden, Behold, I have prepared my dinner: my
oxen and my fatlings are killed, and all things are ready: come
unto the marriage. But they made light of it, and went their
ways, one to his farm, another to his merchandise: And the
remnant took his servants, and entreated them spitefully, and
slew them. But when the king heard thereof, he was wroth:
and he sent forth his armies, and destroyed those murderers,
and burned up their city. Then saith he to his servants, The
wedding is ready, but they which were bidden were not
worthy. Go ye therefore into the highways, and as many as
ye shall find, bid to the marriage. So those servants went out
into the highways, and gathered together all as many as they
found, both bad and good: and the wedding was furnished
with guests. And when the king came in to see the guests, he
saw there a man which had not on a wedding garment: And
he saith unto him, Friend, how camest thou in hither not
having a wedding garment? And he was speechless. Then said
the king to the servants, Bind him hand and foot, and take
him away, and cast him into outer darkness; there shall be
weeping and gnashing of teeth. For many are called, but few
are chosen.

Matthew 22:2-14

CHAPTER 14
- W O R K S -

For other foundation can no man lay than that is laid, which is Jesus Christ. Now if any man build upon this foundation gold, silver, precious stones, wood, hay, stubble; Every man's work shall be made manifest: for the day shall declare it, because it shall be revealed by fire; and the fire shall try every man's work of what sort it is. If any man's work abide which he hath built thereupon, he shall receive a reward. If any man's work shall be burned, he shall suffer loss: but he himself shall be saved; yet so as by fire. Know ye not that ye are the temple of God, and that the Spirit of God dwelleth in you? If any man defile the temple of God, him shall God destroy; for the temple of God is holy, which temple ye are.
1 Corinthians 3:11-17

Any good deed, physical labor, humanitarian project, the list is endless; anything that we do or say <u>that is not</u> in direct obedience to the leadership, unction, encouraging by the Holy Spirit will be of no value in eternity. Those "works" done <u>without being told</u> to be done by God speaking directly to us to do and/or say will be burned. It is those "works" that God has <u>specifically told us to do</u>, through His Holy Spirit, and in obedience we do and/or say what He has said, will be stored in heaven, "will receive a reward." Here is an example: It is God's will that we give to the poor, but only to those <u>He tells</u> us to. To give to the poor without being told, is a "work" that "will be burned." If God has told me to give twenty dollars to someone, and I do as <u>He said</u>, I "will receive a reward."

So it is, many Believers busy themselves doing all sorts of good deeds. Although in itself this is good, if God has not said to do any of those things, we are laboring in vain, as far as eternal reward is concerned. Doing these things is GOOD, but God telling us to do and/or say it is BETTER. Multiplied thousands of Believers have done and/or said all kinds of things that have value in the world, but have no eternal value, because God did not tell them do and/or say any of them.

Jesus did nothing for anyone unless the Father told Him to do it. It is like the man at one of the pools of Bethesda who was waiting for an angel to stir the water so he could fall in and be healed; when Jesus found him He healed him. No doubt, Jesus out of compassion, wanted to heal everyone, but His Father only sent Him there for that one person, so afterwards Jesus left, (John 5:2-13). With all this written, those whose works where burned, they being "saved; yet so as by fire" are those Saints who were "working" out of a sense of duty, but not having done so by the directive (*leading*) of the Holy Spirit. The written Word tells us what is God's desire (*chronos*), the Holy Spirit tells us what He requires (*kairos*) from one moment to the next, as we follow and walk with Him out of love for Him and obedience, fulfilling His written word as the Holy Spirit leads, guides, and directs us.

Chapter 15
- L A O D I C E A -

And unto the angel of the church of the Laodiceans write;
These things saith the Amen, the faithful and true witness,
the beginning of the creation of God; I know thy works, that
thou art neither cold nor hot: I would thou wert cold or hot.
So then because thou art lukewarm, and neither cold nor hot,
I will spue thee out of my mouth. Because thou sayest, I am
rich, and increased with goods, and have need of nothing; and
knowest not that thou art wretched, and miserable, and poor,
and blind, and naked: I counsel thee to buy of me gold tried
in the fire, that thou mayest be rich; and white raiment that
thou mayest be clothed, and that the shame of thy nakedness
do not appear; and anoint thine eyes with eyesalve, that thou
mayest see. As many as I love, I rebuke and chasten: be zealous
therefore, and repent. Behold, I stand at the door, and knock:
if any man hear my voice, and open the door, I will come in
to him, and will sup with him, and he with me. To him that
overcometh will I grant to sit with me in my throne, even as I
also overcame, and am set down with my Father in his throne.
He that hath an ear, let him hear what the Spirit saith unto
the churches.

Revelation 3:14-22

Revelation 3:14

And unto the angel of the church of the Laodiceans [just people] write; These things saith the **Amen** [the Yes], [the end] the **faithful and true** witness [His life example], [the middle]

the **beginning** of the creation of God; [the Word] [the beginning]

3:15

I know thy **works,** [physical labor, hard working; the rest of this verse implies He is not concerned with their physical labor, but their lack of diligence toward their spiritual well-being. They were a hard working people for the temporal things, but not for their eternal.]

that thou art neither cold nor hot:

I would thou wert cold or hot.

3:16   **lukewarm does not bring honor or glory to God**

So then because thou art lukewarm, [religious, foolish virgin, hypocrite]

and neither cold nor hot, I will spue thee out of my mouth. [Puts a bad taste in God's mouth, like lukewarm water, unacceptable, like salt that has lost its savor, Matthew 5:13]

3:17

Because thou sayest,

I am rich,

and **increased with goods,**

and **have need of nothing;**

and **knowest not that thou art wretched,**

and **miserable,**

and **poor,**   [God says you are deceived]

and **blind,**

and **naked:**

3:18

I counsel thee to buy of me gold tried in the fire, that thou mayest be rich; [a chastened, perfected life, abundant life, treasure in earthen vessel]

and white raiment, that thou mayest be clothed, and that the shame of thy nakedness do not appear; [God's righteousness, His glory, His glow, His anointing on our life is our garment]

and anoint thine eyes with eyesalve, that thou mayest see. [The Holy Spirit gives us the ability to "see", not what we have learned from others, but that which is revealed to us by God]

3:19

As many as I love, I rebuke and chasten: [chastened that we would not be condemned with the world; chastens every son, peaceable fruit of righteousness...Heb. 12:11; His attention to our best interest to make us acceptable to God shows us His love]

be zealous therefore, and **repent**

3:20

Behold, I stand at the door, and knock: if any man hear my voice, [HIS DESIRE TO FELLOWSHIP WITH US, INTIMACY] and open the door, I will come in to him, and will sup with him, and he with me.

3:21

To him that <u>overcometh</u> [*He will not be ashamed to call us brethren*] will I grant to sit with me in my throne, [*He will take us home to meet His Father, we will reign with Him*] even as I also overcame, and am set down with my Father in his throne.

3:22

He that hath an ear, let him hear what the Spirit saith unto the churches.

God's exhortation to the church of Laodicea is a call of God to those who are Lukewarm in the faith.

The name Laodicea means: "just people". It is obvious by God's description that the Believers were falling short of being "just" in the sight of God. Jesus describes himself as all encompassing, His being the beginning, the standard of His life when He walked the earth **(the faithful and true witness)**, and the One who not only said, "It is finished," but the One with whom God will complete His plan for man (the Judgment). Jesus is the Amen. v.14.

The Greek word for **"works"** v.15 is in reference to physical labor, or occupation. The population of the city prided themselves on their ability to get wealth, and being a hard working people. The city had an abundance of gold. God was not addressing this fact about them, for it was the spiritual condition of the heart He was interested in (obedience or disobedience), **"...thou art neither cold nor hot: I would thou wert cold or hot. So then because thou art lukewarm, and neither cold nor hot, I will spue thee out of my mouth."** These believers were not working hard at developing a deep intimate relationship with God.

> **Charge them that are rich in this world, that they be not highminded, nor trust in uncertain riches, but in the living God, who giveth us richly all things to enjoy; That they do good, that they be rich in good works, ready to distribute, willing to communicate; Laying up in store for themselves a good foundation against the time to come, that they may lay hold on eternal life.**
>
> **1 Timothy 6:17-19**

God has no problem with our working hard and getting financial gain, He even encourages it; not only for personal financial gain, but also for the financial needs of others and the kingdom.

And let ours also learn to maintain good works (*occupation*) **for necessary uses** (*needs*), **that they be not unfruitful** (*pennyless*).
Titus 3:14

And whatsoever ye do, do it heartily, as to the Lord, and not unto men;
Colossians 3:23

Hard work is encouraged even as a testament to the presence of God in our life, not only to co-workers but also to Management. God also requires us to have respect for authority, not being loud, obnoxious, and argumentative, in all not behaving like an unconverted Sinner.

For years I questioned the statement **"I would thou wert cold or hot."** I have come to the understanding that the troubling effect being lukewarm has on God, is that because these type of believers have a heart of interest for the things of God, but not an insatiable desire to comply with His expectations, God's heart is torn over the decision to reject them as His. It is like a parent who has no other choice but to put an adult child out of the house because it would not comply with their authority and rules of conduct. The parent loves the child because of a maternal bond, but will grieve over the decision to put them out. God by His nature cannot tolerate our being lukewarm; blatant disregard for total surrender to do His will this is rebellion. Old Testament Jewish law required that a child bent on rebellion be put to death by stoning (Deuteronomy 21:18-21). As in the natural so it is in the supernatural, **"I will spue thee out of my mouth."**

The Laodicean Christians, and all who are Lukewarm in their faith toward God, being deceived in believing all is well with their relationship with God, boast of being spiritually rich, increased with goods, and having need of nothing, unaware they are in spiritual poverty (wretched, miserable, poor, blind, and naked) v.17. God implores, and pleads with the Lukewarm to set their heart to go deep in their relationship with Him. To go deeper, for He wants to impart to them the riches of His knowledge and wisdom; His hidden riches, pearls, and mysteries, revelation that will astonish. He wants to place upon them His righteousness, glory, and an overwhelming prevailing anointing on their life. An anointing that not only has a positive effect on their own life, but also on the lives of those they would come in contact with, (*Isaiah 58:8-14*).

We can not walk in blatant disobedience, in the way of sinners, and think God will not require it of us (discipline). For, He will not let us live out our newness of life that way." God does not turn His back on the Hypocrite, Religious, Lukewarm, and even the Backslider, but will do whatever is necessary to get them to repent of their rebellion, and unacceptable standard of obedience. He says, **"As many as I love, I rebuke and chasten: be zealous therefore, and repent."** v.19

It is His attention to our best interest, to make our walk with Him acceptable, that demonstrates His love for us. Some of the ways He will discipline us is through our finances, relationships, our health, and anything else to get our attention that He requires a "high standard" of conduct or behavior. **God allows difficulties and bad experiences to happen to us to draw us closer to Him, not to cause us to abandon Him.** The lifespan of our humanity is short, compared to eternity, therefore God says to the Lukewarm, **"be zealous therefore, and repent,"** passionately pursue me, and do not procrastinate.

> **Labour not for the meat which perisheth, but for that meat which endureth unto everlasting life, which the Son of man shall give unto you: for him hath God the Father sealed.**
> **John 6:27**

> **The labour of the righteous tendeth to life: the fruit of the wicked to sin** (*death*).
> **Proverbs 10:16**

"Behold, I stand at the door, and knock: if any man hear my voice, and open the door, I will come in to him, and will sup with him, and he with me." v.20 This is God's desire for us, to have fellowship with Him, to build upon an intimate relationship with Him, and to fulfill His every expectation of us. This is like a final word to all of the churches, and more specifically every individual believer in the church, no matter what is the condition of their relationship with Him that spans across the centuries.

God created mankind, all other reasons aside, to have a creation He could fellowship with. I would suppose that is why He said, "...Let us make man in our image, after our likeness...Gen. 1:26." I would say this to be a fact also, because of how much time God spent with Adam.

After Adam and Eve sinned, God provided atonement for their sin so that the fellowship could be restored. From Adam until this day God has spoken to men and women for various reasons, but I believe one of the reasons has been to fellowship with us. How awesome is this, and how blessed I feel when I consider that just as God had fellowship with Adam He chooses to fellowship with ME. Of course not just with me, but also with all of those who desire to obey Him with all of their heart, mind, soul, and strength, and are consistently doing it.

God desires a people who are perfect in heart, whose heart is set on him, **FERVENTLY**. I have shared that all being "perfect" in the sight of God is, is to obey His spoken word. The **written word** of God paves the way to bring us to the place where we can hear God speak to us the **spoken word**, and to be able to discern that it is Him and not another voice. It is through the spoken word that we can know God's specific desires for us as an individual.

The bible does not go into detail about how much time pasted before Adam was finished with all of the duties God gave him to do up to the day Adam and Eve sinned. Knowing that God desires an intimated relationship with His children, I could see God spending a lot of time with Adam and Eve. Although it is obvious to me that after Adam and Eve sinned, God went looking for them to provide an atonement for their sin, I am prone to wonder if God went looking for them with the intent of fellowshipping with them, as if it was something He had done on a regular basis. **God's desire to fellowship with His children is insatiable.**

God is not willing that any would perish but that **ALL** would come to repentance (2 Peter 3:9). Obviously, because He wants to be mankind's Father and not just mankind's Creator, but what if also because He wants to fellowship with mankind? Without redemption we cannot have fellowship with Him. He has established **REDEMPTION** to be a prerequisite. With the open dialog of fellowship, comes the revealing of His innumerable hidden mysteries, personality, and character. The Lord, our Father, our Daddy, and our Friend who sticks closer than a brother loves us so much.

Having created man after His own likeness, and in His image, we have been created to fellowship with Him on His level. God comes down to our level to save us. When the work of salvation has been completed in our heart and His Holy Spirit dwells in us, through the Holy Spirit by faith we have access to God's throne, and His throne room to fellowship with Him were He dwells in the heavenliness. **Instead of Jesus standing at the door of our heart wanting to come in to fellowship with us, He has made it possible for us to stand at the door of his throne room wanting to come in and fellowship with Him.**

If after receiving Jesus into our heart, the full riches of His mercy and grace, we choose to be content living the lifestyle of nominal-Christianity, which is a casual nonchalant walk with God (*Lukewarm*), we will never know what it is to fellowship with Him. <u>It is with a dedicated sincere attempt to know Him in the fullness of His personality and character, fueled by obeying His perfect will for our life, that will make it possible for us to fellowship with Him on His level.</u> God is not pleased with a lifestyle of nominal-Christianity, which borderlines a dead religious attempt to be a Christian. God's plea to those who fall into this category is, **"Move up higher, there is so much more about Me that you have yet to experience.**

The door that Jesus is knocking on (v.20) is the one that is found in the heart of those who profess to be his people. He is saying, **"I want to have fellowship with you, the intimate kind, that is only found through being one with me".** Therefore He says to us, "I counsel thee to buy of me". Our dying to self-ambitions, self-desires, and self-will makes intimate fellowship with the Lord possible. **"I will sup with him and he with me", is a fellowship with God, Jesus, and the Holy Spirit no words can adequately describe.** It is a fellowship that must be experienced to understand. Being One with God opens the door to the intimate fellowship God wants to have with us.

In Jesus' final statement to the church of Laodicea, which is a word to the Lukewarm, and equally to the Hypocrite, Religious, and Backslider, **"To him that overcometh** (to him that will yield to My counsel, be zealous and repent, to seek after me with all their heart, mind, soul, strength) **will I grant to sit with me in my throne, even as I also overcame, and am set down with my Father in his throne."** v. 21. If we choose to resist Him, rebel, and be contentious, to say in our heart, "I will not have this man to rule over me", not only will His chastening be upon us, but so will His wrath, even to the eternal ruin of our soul, if we do not repent of our rebellion.

He said therefore, A certain nobleman went into a far country to receive for himself a kingdom, and to return. And he called his ten servants, and delivered them ten pounds, and said unto them, Occupy till I come. But his citizens hated him, and sent a message after him, saying, We will not have this man to reign over us...But those mine enemies, which would not that I should reign over them, bring hither, and slay them before me.

Luke 19:12-14, 27

CHAPTER 16
~ PROPHETS ~

And Moses said unto him, Enviest thou for my sake? Would God that all the Lord's people were prophets, and that the LORD would put his spirit upon them!

Numbers 11:29

Saying, touch not mine anointed and do my prophets no harm.

1 Chronicles 16:22

Touch not mine anointed and do my prophets no harm is a warning from God to those who would harm any of God's people. Although this particular scripture has significance for the people of the nation of Israel because of the promises made to their forefathers, it has no less significance to those who are of spiritual Israel (Christians whether they be Jew or Gentile), for true Israel are those who have had their heart circumcised by the Holy Spirit. As true born again Christians we are as much God's anointed as a Prophet.

For he is not a Jew, which is one outwardly; neither is that circumcision, which is outward in the flesh: But he is a Jew, which is one inwardly; and circumcision is that of the heart, in the spirit, and not in the letter; whose praise is not of men, but of God.

Romans 2:28-29

Circumcise therefore the foreskin of your heart, and be no more stiff necked.
Deuteronomy 10:16

And the Lord thy God will circumcise thine heart, and the heart of thy seed, to love the Lord thy God with all thine heart, and with all thy soul, that thou mayest live.
Deuteronomy 30:6

Would God that all the Lord's people were prophets, is a call of God to His church today. It is not so much that His desire is to use all of us to prophesy, as much as it is His desire that we walk in what I call "revival status", walking a lifestyle of total obedience to His perfect will, satisfying all requirements of His desires and his alone for our behavior and life endeavors. God's desire is for all of us who make up His true church to live the consecrated life of a faithful and true Prophet, called of God to speak for Him and to live lives that prove to those who are unsaved, that there is a God that loves them beyond their comprehension, and that we are living proof of this fact.

If when a lost soul sees us and there is not enough of a radical difference in our conduct and endeavors to cause them to say, there is something different about you, are you a Christian, we are living below God's standard for our life? Jesus said of himself in Revelation 3:14 "... **the faithful and true witness.**" Worldliness and a false spirit of religion prevail in the church worldwide. Worldliness and carnality, prevailing in the life a person who claims to be a Christian, cause many who are unsaved to critically say, "If that is what being a Christian is all about I don't want any part of it."

The foolish virgins of Matthew 25:3, are those who profess to be Christians, but do not have the power and anointing of the Holy Spirit. This endowment of power has also all of the Gifts of the Holy Spirit attached to it, which make the Holy Spirit filled Christian a candidate for God to use for the operation of any of the Gifts of the Holy Spirit as He wills, at any given point in time, to make His presence known; not only for the encouragement of the Saints, but also for the radical life changing born again experience of lost souls. **Without the Holy Spirit we can never live the standard that God desires for us,** nor can we know what is happening on a supernatural level, what is about to happen in the near future, in the natural level.

Through the Holy Spirit God reveals to us His secrets, His hidden agenda, to those who are His people, spiritual Israel. It is because of not having this endowment of power, that comes with being "filled with the Holy Spirit", that has caused many well meaning but incorrectly informed preachers, to preach for centuries that we can not live a sinless life. Every provision for living without sin is provided for God's people through and by the Holy Spirit. The same Holy Spirit that dwelt in Jesus, for Him to live a sinless life, now dwells in a Holy Spirit filled Christian to help us to obey God to the same degree as Jesus did. God's word tells us that we are to follow in the steps of Jesus who knew no sin, and that those who have the Spirit of God in them cannot sin.

For even hereunto were ye called: because Christ also suffered for us, leaving us an example, <u>that ye should follow his steps:</u> <u>Who knew no sin</u>, neither was guile found in his mouth:
1 Peter 2:21-22

Whosoever is born of God doth not commit sin; for his seed remaineth in him: and he cannot sin, because he is born of God.
1 John 3:9

Surely the Lord will do nothing, but he revealeth his secret unto his servant the prophets.
Amos 3:7

But as it is written, Eye hath not seen, nor ear heard, neither have entered into the heart of man, the things which God hath prepared for them that love him. <u>But God hath revealed them unto us by his Spirit</u>: for the Spirit searcheth all things, yea, the deep things of God.
1 Corinthians 2:9-10

Perfection in the sight of God is this: Not disobeying God. If we cannot hear God speak to us, how can we know what He wants us to do? **The Holy Spirit gives us the ability to hear God speak, and the**

endowment of power gives us the ability to do what He says. When we hear God speak to us, and we do what He says, this is what makes us His children. The written word of God is given to instruct us about God, a glimpse into His personality and character, and so much more.

The written word is never intended by God to be the end of knowing about Him; it is only the beginning. God wants to speak to us on a personal level through His Holy Spirit. As He does with the Prophets so He does with all of those who are of the "household of faith".

For as many as are led by the Spirit of God, they are the sons of God

Romans 8:14

What man is he that feareth the Lord? him shall he teach in the way that he shall choose.

Psalm 25:12

An unsaved person has no concept of what being filled with the Holy Spirit is about and neither does a person who calls him or herself a Christian who lives as worldly a lifestyle as an unsaved person. I am of the persuasion that believers, who call him or herself a Christian and cusses like a sinner and behaves like one, if in truth they are a Christian, does so because they are not filled with the power of the Holy Spirit to live and behave any other way. According the Matthew 25:12 such a believer is a foolish virgin, who when the Lord comes will not be worthy to go with Him, hearing Him say, "Verily I say unto you, I know you not." **Living a fully obedient life before God is a maturing process that takes the endowment of power, that accompanies the in filling of the Holy Spirit, God's anointing upon our lives, to be able to do his perfect will for our life.**

The need of the world today is crying out for the true children of God to live the example of Christ in their lives, to be tangible proof of the truth and reality that there is a God in heaven and in the world today. The world is wanting proof, that there is actually a Son of God, who lived, died for our sins, and rose from the grave with power and majesty, to signify to the world, that by virtue of His resurrection, He alone has been declared with power, that He is the Son of God and the only hope for the salvation of humanity, (Romans 1:4, 8:19).

How will the world know, unless all of us who make up the true body of Christ, repent of our slothfulness, slumber, deadness of spirit, and playing church, to be about doing Father's business, (His desires and His alone)? We cannot begin to win the world to Christ, nor even our community, nor neighbors; except we die that they might live. **We must become One with God.** The way we do this is to continually do what Jesus Christ "the Son of man" did. "And being found in fashion as a man, He humbled Himself and became obedient...Phil. 2:8."

As Jesus said of Himself in Revelation 3:14 "**...the faithful and true witness.**" We are incapable of being a faithful and true witness without the endowment of power that is given to us when we are filled with the Holy Spirit. There are two operations of the Holy Spirit. When having repented of our sins, to accept Jesus as Lord and Savior of our life, the Holy Spirit enters into our heart to give to us the born again experience. As a prayer is what it took for us to receive the new birth, so it takes a prayer for us to receive the endowment of power, which comes with being filled with the Holy Spirit.

> **And when Paul had laid his hands upon them, the Holy Ghost came on them; and they spake with tongues, and prophesied.**
>
> **Acts 19:6**

> **<u>Who, when they were come down, prayed for them, that they might receive the Holy Ghost</u>: (For as yet he was fallen upon none of them: only they were baptized in the name of the Lord Jesus.) <u>Then laid they their hands on them, and they received the Holy Ghost</u>.**
>
> **Acts 8:15-17**

Although prayer and the laying on of hands is how some receive the Holy Ghost, the Holy Spirit can be received by praying on our own to receive the endowment of power and the Gifts of the Holy Spirit that accompany the in filling of the Holy Ghost. Having had first hand experience, prior the my own conversion, of seeing and hearing those who had the gift of the Holy Spirit (a prayer language), praying and worshiping God with the language He gave them, I desired to have the gift myself. The day I gave my heart to Jesus, I prayed to receive the experience myself.

The way God gave the gift to me began with three words in my mind. It is because of my receiving the gift this way that I believed I had thought those words up, not that it was God who gave them to me. It was only after a week later that I asked the Christian, who was used of God to guide me in the direction of my own conversion to Jesus, to pray for me to receive the Holy Spirit, when she prayed nothing happened. I then told her (now my sister-in-law) about the three words. God gave her the confirmation that I had the gift of the Holy Spirit. At first I refused to believe her, saying, I thought those three words up, she insisted I had the gift, I said, I'll show you. I said the three words again, but this time many more words followed after those three words, which didn't enter my mind. I didn't need anymore convincing.

It is because of my own experience, when I pray for others to receive the gift, I pray for the Lord to put a few words in their mind to help them get started. I am aware that not everyone needs this, but just like me, some do. I also know that the Holy Spirit has various ways to gift us. Many have experienced a lump like feeling in their throat, before they let the words out. When anyone experiences receiving the gift of the Holy Spirit this way, if all you can do is grown, stammer, or shout just do it and don't hold back for fear or because you don't want to embarrass yourself; such feelings are a ploy of the Enemy, to hinder you from receiving the Holy Spirit.

The Enemy knows a Christian filled with the Holy Spirit is a significant threat to him and his wicked devices. In every account in the book of Acts, whether specifically mentioned or implied, a God given language followed being filled with the Holy Spirit. It is because of the five references given in the book of Acts, where Christians received the Holy Spirit, and a prayer language ensued, that it is believed that receiving a prayer language is given by God as proof to everyone present, as well as ourselves, that a Christian has receive the Holy Spirit and the endowment of power to be an effective and powerful witness for God. I can say also, the ability to be a "faithful and true witness", just like Jesus Christ.

But ye shall receive power, after that the Holy Ghost is come upon you: and ye shall be witnesses unto me both in Jerusalem, and in   all Judaea, and in Samaria, and unto the uttermost part of the earth.

Acts 1:8.

And there appeared unto them cloven tongues like as of fire, and it sat upon each of them. And they were all filled with the Holy Ghost, and began to speak with other tongues, as the Spirit gave them utterance.

Acts 2:3-4

Here is the patience of the saints: here are they that keep the commandments of God, and the faith of Jesus.

Revelation 14:12

There are those who have been taught that the gift and gifts of the Holy Spirit are not for today, causing Christians who are not filled with the Holy Spirit to erroneously believe many false doctrines about this Pentecost experience, and to avoid being filled with the Holy Spirit altogether, teaching that this experience was received at conversion, a doctrine the bible does not confirm. The Enemy has also been able to cause the gift of the Holy Spirit to be despised, using abuse or misuse of the prayer language (tongues as the bible refers to the gift). The revival of the early 1900's began because God began to endow Christians with the gift of the Holy Spirit, to become powerful witnesses for Him throughout the world. The Enemy used an erroneous doctrine and the many abuses of the gifts, to discourage many Christians from receiving the gifts and power of the Holy Spirit for themselves, with the intent of keeping God's church powerless. **Rise up O child of God, refuse to wallow in the pig pin of spiritual weakness, and become a force against the Enemy to be reckoned with!**

RISE UP O MEN OF GOD

Rise up O men of God! Have done with lesser things, give heart and mind and soul and strength to serve the King of Kings. Rise up, O men of God! His kingdom tarries long; bring in the brotherhood and end the night of wrong. Rise up, O men of God! The church for you doth wait. Her strength unequal to her task; rise up, and make her great! Lift high the cross of Christ! Tread where His feet have trod; as brothers of the Son of man, rise up, O men of God!

Without the endowment of power, received with the gift of the Holy Spirit, the Church is unequal to her task. To make God's church great, takes God working through us. A consecrated life of total obedience to God, and separation from all worldliness and a religious spirit full of all its carnal stench, coupled with the power of the Holy Spirit makes it possible for us to pillage ruthlessly the kingdom of darkness, and take territory for Christ.

There is confusion among many who have a prayer language (tongues), which is given when a Christian receives the Holy Spirit, that this gift of tongues requires interpretation. Our spirit operates this gift of tongues not the Holy Spirit therefore no interpretation is needed. When we are filled with the Holy Spirit God gives our spirit the ability to speak in another language, this ability we were not taught but was given to use by God. This gift is controlled by us, and can be initiated whenever we desire to speak in this God given language, for the purpose of praying about something we have no idea how to word a prayer for, or to sing and voice praises to God. I do not know what I am saying, nor does anyone who hears me, for it is a personal conversation between God and me.

For if I pray in an unknown tongue my spirit prayeth, but my understanding is unfruitful. What is it then? I will pray with the spirit, and I will pray with the understanding also; I will sing with the spirit, and I will sing with the understanding also.
1 Corinthians 14:14-15

When Paul was writing to the Corinthian church about the gifts of the Holy Spirit, there were abuses happening for which he had to give certain instruction to cause the abuses to cease, but in no way did he instruct them to forfeit the using of the gift or gifts of the Holy Spirit. Paul having inserted the information about prayer and singing in this fourteenth chapter, the concept of praying and praising by our spirit is misunderstood by many to imply that the God given prayer language is God speaking and needs an interpretation, when it is not Him speaking. The gift of tongues that the Holy Spirit moves on us, to give a message to the church, does need the gift of interpretation, a gift that the Holy

Spirit will operate through the same person or someone else of His own choosing.

When the Holy Spirit is moving in a service to manifest any of the nine gifts of the Holy Spirit through His people, many who are sensing God manifesting Himself this way, can mistaken He is wanting to use them, when actually He is not. This is why a Spirit filled Christian needs to test the anointing they are feeling to see if it is actually God wanting to use them, or that they are just getting "caught up in the moment". It is a lack of correct discernment that Paul was trying to instruct the Corinthian church about, having written this statement also:

And the spirits of the prophets are subject to the prophets
1 Corinthians 14:33

A person may ask, what is the need for the gift of tongues anyway, what is the significance? The fourteenth chapter of Corinthians answers this question, stating in verse 22 that tongues are for a sign. The word "sign" implying the presence and existence of God, Paul says of the gift given to us for prayer and praise:

He that speaketh in an unknown tongue edifieth himself;....
1 Corinthians 14:4a

Edify means build, used in this scripture if means a maturing force among other positive effects, the building of our faith. The prayer language is a benefit God has given to us to help perfect us. There is an obvious difference that can be seen in a Christian who has the Holy Spirit, as has been discussed, and a Christian who does not. Worldliness and carnality abound in varying degrees, in the life of the Christian without the Holy Spirit and **obvious defeat**. In the life of a Christian who has the Holy Spirit there is **evident victory** over worldliness and carnality; the varying degree of victory is determined by our willingness to access the power to be 100 percent victorious over a desire of the flesh to disobey God. With this fact I can restate what is written in this document:

"A consecrated life of total obedience to God, and separation from all worldliness and a religious spirit full of all its carnal stench, coupled with the power of the Holy Spirit makes it possible for us

to pillage ruthlessly the kingdom of darkness, and take territory for Christ".

Why continue to let the enemy keep you bound in a life of worldliness and carnality, when God has provided through the infilling of the Holy Spirit the way of escape and the **leap forward** to intimate fellowship with God in the throne room of His presence, the heavenly places in Christ, that can only be accessed with the help of the Holy Spirit? If you do not have the Holy Spirit, the endowment of power, and the gifts of the Holy Spirit being manifest in and through your life, **do not let the lies of the "foolish virgins" who choose not to believe what His word says** keep you from the victory, power, and intimate relationship God wants to have with you. Ask Him to fill you with His Holy Spirit.

Don't be one of the foolish virgins who were not allowed to enter into the marriage feast. Matthew 25:11-12... **Afterward came also the other virgins, saying, Lord, Lord, open to us. But he answered and said; Verily I say unto you, I know you not.** Prophets have an intimate relationship with God. All who are filled with the Holy Spirit are God's present day prophets to whom He reveals His secrets, His personality and character, those who have intimate fellowship with Him, who can hear His voice and obey.

CHAPTER 17
~ OBEDIENCE, BEING ONE WITH GOD ~

Many Christians, not all, have experienced "**walking in the Spirit**" at one time or another, during their lifetime in Christ. The problem, with the majority of the Saints, who have experienced this deep walk with Christ, is they have not continued in it. Rather, they became "**forgetful hearers**," in turn causing them to fall back into "**nominal-Christianity**," such Christianity that is extremely displeasing to God, and continually grieves the Holy Spirit...who we are commanded not to grieve, (Eph. 4:30).

The Lord has shown me that 90%, more or less, of the true born-again believers, are not walking in heavenly places in Christ. They think, just because they are endeavoring to press toward the mark, or endeavoring to live for Christ, or trying to draw closer to God, or drawing closer to God, they are walking in heavenly places, or just by virtue of the fact that they are Christians. When in reality, they are missing the "**mark**", and don't even realize it. According to Ephesians 5:14 they are asleep, dead, and without light. (Not without Christ, for they are definitely saved, but without light).

Those who walk in heavenly places in Christ are not trying to get closer to God, but they are actually and altogether close to God, One with Him and He One with us, "**.... but he that is joined unto the Lord is one Spirit... 1 Cor. 6:17**." Paul the Apostle continually walked in heavenly places in Christ Jesus. Those who are close to God, they who are continually <u>one</u> with Him, are those who "**press**" toward the mark, and are those who in all truth "die daily." What do those who truly "**die daily**," die daily to, all of their desires and affections?

> **And they that are Christ's have crucified the flesh with the affections and lusts** (*desires*). **If we live in the Spirit, let us also walk in the Spirit.**
>
> **Galatians 5:24-25**

Notice, it is possible to live in the Spirit, but not walk in the Spirit. Those who have crucified the flesh are those who walk in the Spirit. Those Saints who live after their own will, whether in part or totally, to please or fulfill some or all of their desires, live in the Spirit, but seldom, if at all, walk the Spirit. The Saints who commit sin are not walking 100% of the time in the Spirit, although they live in the Spirit.

> **Whosoever is born of God doth not commit sin; for His seed remaineth in him; and he cannot sin, because he is born of God.**
>
> **1 John 3:9**

Those who continually walk 100% of the time in the Spirit do not commit sin.

Satan and his devils are angry about what is written herein, and for what I have set myself to do, to expose a truth that is desperately needed and expected by God, to be accomplished and followed in the life of every Saint of God. The major majority of Saints have been lullabied into a spiritual slumber of self-deception to the point where, they think they understand what I am trying to tell them. What I am trying to convey is extremely deep and spiritual, Only those who are in all reality and truth, "**pressing toward the mark**," as Paul did, can truly understand what I am writing about.

This doctrine is so little known or understood by the major majority of Saints and Preachers today, that it can almost be labeled a lost doctrine of the very heart of the epistles and books of the New Testament. Listen to what is said of Jesus:

> **And being found in fashion as a man, he humbled himself and became obedient unto death, even the death of the cross.**
>
> **Philippians 2:8**

Although Jesus as the Son of God is perfect, Jesus the Son of Man had to learn obedience (Hebrews 5:8), and be made perfect (Hebrews 2:10). The way He accomplished this was by **"dying daily,"** (everyday, all His life), to His own will and desires, to do the Father's will only. Why was Jesus' life a sinless life? Not only because He is the Son of God, but also for the reason that, **"He humbled Himself and became obedient."**

What Jesus learned as the Son of Man, He passed on to us, through His "holy apostles and prophets" in the New Testament; but the eyes of the Saints have been blinded by the drive to fulfill some or all of their own ambitions and desires, rather than all and only God's. The major majority of Christians (90% more of less) are so blinded, because of their own will, that they miss this truth in their daily reading and study of the scriptures. They think they understand what they read, but in reality, they are blind and without light, I'm not talking about religious folk, I'm talking about true, everyday, born again believers... Christians.

I was also blinded, but now I can truly see, and with this sight has come a unity and oneness with Christ and Father, that very few Saints have experienced. **Yet, it is within the reach of every one of us, if only we will seek the revealing of this truth from God, then receive it and run with it, (pursue it with all our life,** Mark 12:30). This is a dying that others might live. What others, those who are without Christ and dead in trespasses and sin; but not only they, the brethren also?

The Lord has shown me, that there are sinners who will never give their lives to Jesus, except we lead them into salvation. The Lord has revealed to me that, by our disobedience, instead of **totally dying out to "self,"** we hinder, and possibly could prevent them from ever giving their life to Christ. How disturbing! This means, our disobedience to the "**perfect will of God**" could, and may have already caused, a soul to perish in hell forever, with their blood being required at our hands. Anything less than obeying God's "**perfect will**" is total disobedience, rebellion, and sin.

Why did the church of the Apostles bring souls to Christ by the hundreds, and some by the thousands? One reason is, because the Apostles, being examples of total death to self-ambitions and desires, stirred their converts to Christ, to follow the same example of full obedience. For their total commitment, God endowed the Saints with such a effective witness, life, and testimony that sinners swarmed to the "alter" of salvation. That alter being Jesus Christ. Thank God... hallelujah! What caused the great revivals in America during the 1800's and the early 1900's to fill many of the churches of this country with true believers? Partly, the preachers, who preached those revivals, learned the art of dying, that others would live.

How did Jesus purchase eternal life for us? He died for our offenses and was raised again for our justification (Romans 4:25). How will these sinners, who I have mentioned ever receive this same eternal life, we have received in Christ? We must learn how to die that they may live, and learn how to die for others to live.

My battle is no longer a matter of drawing closer to God, but rather to stay close to Him and be conformed to the image of His Son, which God cannot begin to effectively do, in our life, until we are close to Him, and stay there. This is walking in heavenly places in Christ Jesus. There is a kingdom of difference between drawing closer to God and being close to God, but only when we stay close to Him. Hear Jesus' prayer for us:

And for their sakes I sanctify myself that they also might be sanctified through the truth. Neither pray I for these alone, but for them also which shall believe on me through their word; that they all may be one; as thou, Father art in me and I in thee, that they also may be one in us: that the world may believe that thou hast sent me.

John 17:19-21

Has God answered His prayer? Yes, but only in the life of those who throughout the centuries have yielded, as Jesus the "Son of man" yielded all, to God's full desires and expectations, for their lives. These Saints, God has used, and is continuing to use, such as these, today, to turn or begin to turn, the world "right side up" for Christ. My words are so feeble, when trying to convey the depth, reality, and truth about what I have tried, in few words, but not fully succeeded, the truth, about how very few Christians actually please God and walk in heavenly places in Christ Jesus.

Many Christians have yet to know what being One with God is really like, and continue moment by moment to be One with Him. As I have written, **"...it is within the reach of everyone of us, if only we will seek the revealing of this truth from God, then receive it and run** with it, (pursue it with all our life)." God cannot effectively use us, as He desires, until we die totally to our desires to do His only and always; when we do this continually, it causes us to become One with Him and He One with us.

The Lord has shown me how I can be One with Him, as well as how to continue to be One with Him, I call it **"continual fasting."** Sounds simple doesn't it? But, O the blessedness! Not only this but also the great help of God that is bestowed on me, and the mighty power of God that is manifested in and through my life, which gives me the full ability to not only be One with God, but also continue to be One with Him. It is difficult for me to clearly and simply tell you what has been happening in my soul, but how tremendous the jubilation. There is a continual joy in my voice and tone of rejoicing in my life, which I have even yet the more to experience. I am persuaded of God, that I will experience it.

My definition of continual fasting is, fasting more than eating, which is fasting everyday, whether all day or part of the day. I am not talking about dieting or a matter of missing some meals, I am talking about actually and all altogether fasting. If I would stop this, it would signal the beginning of my departure from this wonderful place of total fellowship and Oneness, I experience in the Spirit with Father.

RISE UP O MEN OF GOD

Rise up O men of God! Have done with lesser things, give heart and mind and soul and strength to serve the King of Kings. Rise up, O men of God! His kingdom tarries long; bring in the brotherhood and end the night of wrong. Rise up, O men of God! The church for you doth wait. Her strength unequal to her task; rise up, and make her great! Lift high the cross of Christ! Tread where His feet have trod; as brothers of the Son of man, rise up, O men of God!

The need of the world today is crying out for the true children of God to live the example of Christ in their lives, to be tangible proof of the truth and reality that there is a God in heaven and in the world today. The world is wanting proof, that there is actually a Son of God, who lived, died for our sins, and rose from the grave with power and majesty, to signify to the world, that by virtue of His resurrection, He alone has been declared with power, that He is the Son of God and the only hope for the salvation of humanity, (Romans 1:4, 8:19). How will the world know, unless all of us who make up the true body of Christ, repent of our slothfulness, slumber, deadness of spirit, and playing church, to be about doing Father's business, (His desires and His alone)?

We cannot begin to win the world to Christ, nor even our community, nor neighbors; except we die that they might live. **We must become One with God.** The way we do this, is to continually do what Jesus Christ "the Son of man" did, "And being found in fashion as a man, He humbled Himself and became obedient...Phil. 2:8."

The Lord gave me a song in 1973 titled, "He shined His life in our hearts." The third stanza follows the title with these words,

> So to employ to please our Lord
> To tell men of His wondrous love
> His changing power revealed in us

This is definitely true, and being accomplished in and through those who are One with God and continue to be One with Him. Amen!

OBEDIENCE
Walking in heavenly places, being One with God

If we say that we have fellowship with Him, and walk in darkness we lie, and do not the truth; but if we walk in the light, as He is in the light, we have fellowship one with another, and the blood of Jesus Christ His Son cleanseth us from all sin.

1 John 1:6-7

Disobedience breaks our fellowship with God, therefore in order to have fellowship with Him we must be totally obedient, or "**walk in the light.**" The only way we can walk in the light as He is in the light is, to be fully obedient, also by doing this total obedience our body will be full of light.

The light of the body is the eye: If therefore thine eye be single, thy whole body shall be full of light. But if thine eye be evil,

132

**thy whole body shall be full of darkness. If therefore the light
that is in thee be darkness, how great is that darkness?**
Matthew 6:22-23

Therefore, when we walk in the light, the light lives in us. Without
total obedience to God, rather than being full of light, our bodies will
be contaminated with darkness. The degree, to which our bodies will
possess darkness, is determined by the degree of our disobedience to
God's desires and expectations for our life. We are bought with a price...
the blood of Jesus Christ...therefore we are not our own anymore, but
rather God's. **One of God's foremost desires and expectations for us
is, total obedience to His will.** Anything less than full obedience will
mean judgment.

**For whether we live, we live unto the Lord; and whether we
die, we die unto the Lord; whether we live therefore, or die,
we are the Lord's.**
Romans 14:8

**Yet if any man suffer as a Christian, let him not be ashamed;
but let him glorify God on this behalf. For the time is come
that judgment must begin at the house of God; and if it first
begin at us, what shall the end be of them that obey not the
gospel of God? And if the righteous scarcely be saved where
shall the ungodly and the sinner appear?**
1 Peter 4:16-18

**But when we are judged, we are chastened of the Lord, that
we should not be condemned with the world.**
1 Corinthians 11:32

**What know ye not that your body is the temple of the Holy
Ghost which is in you, which ye have of God, and ye are not
your own? For ye are bought with a price; therefore glorify
God in your body, and in your spirit, which are God's.**
1 Corinthians 6:19-20

For if we sin wilfully after that we have received the knowledge of the truth, there remaineth no more sacrifice for sins, but a certain fearful looking for of judgment and fiery indignation, which shall devour the adversaries.

Hebrews 10:26

How can we glorify God in our body and in our spirit escaping chastening or judgment from the Lord? By letting the light that is within us, shine before men.

Let your light so shine before men, that they may see your good works and glorify your Father which is in heaven.

Mathew 5:16

The way this light shines, goes back to the eye being single, which is total obedience to God's desires and expectations, not our own. This obedience to God's will alone is our good works, that people see, which causes our Father to be glorified. Sinners are drawn to Christ as a result of obedience. One act of obedience is to witness to sinners when God directs. When God leads in witnessing, we can look forward to leading the sinner into a born again experience. One of the greatest things, a sinner looks for in a Christian, is total obedience to God; without which we could not be very effective when witnessing.

Here is part of a prayer Jesus prayed for us:

That they all may be one; as thou, father, art in me and I in thee, that they also may be one in us: that the world may believe that thou hast sent me.

John 17:21

The major way we become One with God is, total obedience to His will, and His only.

An added note to witnessing: When God does direct us to witness to an individual we should make it our primary business to do exactly that.

> So thou, O son of man, I have set thee a watchman unto the
> house of Israel; therefore thou shalt hear the word at my
> mouth, and warn them from me. When I say unto the wicked,
> O wicked man, thou shalt surely die; if thou dost not speak
> to warn the wicked from his way, that wicked man shall die in
> his iniquity; but his blood will I require at thine hand.
>
> Ezekiel 33:7-8

There are definitely penalties for not obeying God. As grievous as this may sound, for a Christian a penalty for disobedience is not grievous, it's joyous. Why, for the reason that, chastening brings forth righteousness in our life? Although a spanking doesn't seem joyous at the time it is given, the results are transcending joy.

> Furthermore we have had father's of our flesh which corrected
> us, and we gave them reverence: shall we not much rather be
> in subjection unto the Father of spirits, and live? For they
> verily for a few days chastened us after their own pleasure; but
> he for our profit, that we might be partakers of His holiness.
> Now no chastening for the present seemeth to be joyous, but
> grievous: nevertheless afterward it yieldeth the peaceable fruit
> of righteousness unto them which are exercised thereby.
>
> Hebrews 12:9-11

A number of months ago, the Lord showed me how that our own will blinds, as well as deprives, us of many of the wonderful blessings and truths about His word and the Kingdom of God, that He wants to give and reveal to us. What will follow this paragraph will be in reference to this blindness and being a forgetful hearer.

2 Peter 1:3-10

3. According as His divine power hath given unto us all things
   that pertain unto life and godliness, through the knowledge
   of Him that hath called us to glory and virtue:

In this verse, God says, he has given to us all things that pertain unto life and godliness, as a result of our having given our life to Christ. God has given us every provision, promise, and principle necessary, for us, to be 100% victorious over the sinful and carnal nature of the flesh, when the same Holy Spirit that dwelt in Jesus also dwells in us, to give us the same power, and ability, to overcome sin in our flesh. Therefore, when we stand before our Father, at Judgment, we will not have any excuse acceptable for having sinned. (Romans 6:11-16, 8:11)

4. **Whereby are given unto us exceeding great and precious promises: that by these ye might be partakers of the divine nature, having escaped the corruption that is in the world through lust.**

Notice that in this verse he said, that by virtue of these promises we "might" be partakers of the divine nature. The Lord has shown me that those who totally obey His every desire and expectation <u>will</u> be partakers of the divine nature, and have every right for all the promises to be fulfilled in their life, because we have escaped the corruption that is in the world, which through the lust of the flesh we would be partakers of. When we do not totally obey God, we not only partake of the corruption that is in the world through lust, but fall into the category of the "might be."

5. **And besides this, giving all diligence, add to your faith virtue; and to virtue knowledge;**
6. **And to knowledge temperance; and to temperance patience; and to patience godliness;**
7. **And to godliness brotherly kindness; and brotherly kindness charity.**

All these fruits were accomplished in and through Jesus Christ to perfection. **Therefore, having been left an exhortation to follow in his steps, He who knew no sin (1 Peter 2:21-22), we are to obey God to the same extreme.** When we obey God in all things, we will be walking in the light as God is in the light, having fellowship with Him. This place of fellowship with God is walking in heavenly places, and because of our total obedience to Him, the Lord will become totally one with us. When the Father dwells in us, as He did in Jesus, all these fruits will be manifested in and through our life, also to perfection. When we consider the power and glory of God that would be manifested in and through our life to the world and for the brethren, the reason for an exhortation to total obedience to God's desires and expectations becomes very clear.

8. **For if these things be in you, and abound, they make you that ye shall neither be barren nor unfruitful in the knowledge of our Lord Jesus Christ.**

Not only does the power and glory of God manifest Himself, in and through our life, because of the unity we would have with the Father, but as a result of our total obedience to His will alone, we will also have total access to the infinite abundance of His knowledge and wisdom. Not only do we have access to these truths, but also as a result of our deep fellowship and friendship with the Father, He is continually flooding our spiritual minds with these otherwise hidden riches, pearls, and mysteries of God. (John 15:14-15)

9. **But he that lacketh these things is blind, and cannot see afar off, and hath forgotten that he was purged from his old sins.**

The very action that causes us to miss God's wonderful and glorious truths, causing us to be blind, and not able to see afar off, is disobedience. Disobedience follows as a result of becoming "forgetful hearers" of the very work that God began, in our heart, when we repented of our sins, to yield our entire life to Christ, God's leadership and dominion. As the word says, "...hath forgotten that he was purged from his old sins."

When I say, "the very work began", I mean the fire, the compelling drive, the enthusiastic zeal to do God's will and not our own. **The problem with the majority of Saints today, is they have lost their zeal and left their first love, which motivated them to obey God, and Him only.** We forget so easily, and God's cry to the church today is, "Repent, for the kingdom of God is at hand"; "Remember therefore from whence thou art fallen, and repent, and do the first works; or else I will come unto thee quickly, and will remove thy candlestick out of his place, except thou repent. (Revelation 2:5)

10. **Wherefore the rather, brethren, give diligence to make your calling and election sure: for if ye do these things, ye shall never fall:**

11. **For so an entrance shall be ministered unto you abundantly into the everlasting kingdom of our Lord and Saviour Jesus Christ.**

So much can be said, about the rewards for obedience to the perfect will of God, and anything less than doing His perfect will is total disobedience, rebellion, and sin. Full obedience to God's desires and expectations not only promises abundant life in the present, but also eternal life in the presence of God in the future. **Without holiness no man shall see the Lord** (Hebrews 12:14). Therefore we ought to make our calling and election sure; for by totally obeying God, we shall never fall, but always stand strong and victorious against and above all the fiery darts (accusations) of the wicked. For, in our total obedience to God, the wicked will not be able to say any evil thing about us, unless it's a lie. Isn't that what they did to Jesus? Why anything less than to us also?

> **For unto you it is given in the behalf of Christ, not only to believe on Him, but also to suffer for his sake;**
> **Philippians 1:29**

> **Yea, and all that will live godly in Christ Jesus shall suffer persecution.**
> **2 Timothy 3:12**

When we suffer testing, trials, tribulations, temptations, persecutions or similar things, we are being partakers of Christ's sufferings. How wonderful the thought of this should be to us. For, when we suffer as Jesus suffered, at least in whatever areas we suffer as he suffered, we can experience a sense of unity and fellowship with Him.

Beloved, think it not strange concerning the fiery trail which is to try you, as though some strange thing happened unto you: but rejoice, inasmuch as ye are partakers of Christ's

sufferings; that when His glory shall be revealed, ye may be glad also with exceeding joy.

1 Peter 4:12-13

One quality that is manifested in and through our life, as a result of sufferings, whether it is actually physical persecution or simply spiritual persecution (temptations), is obedience to God, which is being "perfect" in His sight. When we obey God we are being perfect. All perfection is in the sight of God is obeying Him.

...to make the captain of their salvation perfect through sufferings, for both he that sanctifieth and they who are sanctified are all of one: for which cause he is not ashamed to call them brethren.

Hebrews 2:10-11

Though he were a son, yet learned he obedience by the things which he suffered; and being made perfect (*having completed God's will*)**, he became the author of eternal salvation unto all them that obey him:**

Hebrews 5:8-9

Once again therefore, based on these scriptures, we not only learn to obey God through chastening, but also as a result of sufferings (temptation, etc.). For example: When I go through a trial or a testing of my faith, God would say, **don't look at the present distress, but rather, toward the blessing, which is waiting for you, at the end of this suffering, if you endure** (be patient). Now, I could either obey this advice, or I could disobey it. I would rather obey, for at the end of every testing, which I have endured, there has always been a blessing, which surpassed the struggle with great joy.

For this is the love of God, that we keep his commandments: and his commandments are not grievous.

1 John 5:3

Looking unto Jesus the author and finisher of our faith who for the joy that was set before him endured the cross,

139

> **despising the shame, and is set down at the right hand of the throne of God.**
>
> **Hebrews 12:2**

Obedience to God is not a grievous duty, but rather a joyous labor; that is, if we truly love God, as so many of us readily say we do. Total obedience to our Father is not an obedience because of demand, but rather out of love and reverence for the One who loves us, died and rose again for us, now at the right hand of God making intercession for us, according to God's will, in our behalf. Definitely so, and **a true Saint of God obeys Him, not because we have to, but because we want to.** The joy that accompanies total obedience to our Father and Being One with Him, having true fellowship with our Creator, is beyond words to describe. This wonderful place of fellowship, and total obedience, is within the reach of every one of us, if only we will seek God for the revealing of how to attain to it, then receive it and run with it.

The whole duty of man is to obey God, to humble ourselves (as Jesus did, Phil. 2:8), **submitting, to walk in full obedience to our Father,** so to have fellowship in the light, as He is in the light, which the Lord desires for us. God's desire for our fellowship though, is not as great as His desire for our joy, which He intended us to continually experience, before we sinned in Adam. **One of the most obvious reasons, why our Father wants us to have a continual abundance of joy, and desires our uninterrupted fellowship, is LOVE.**

> **Let us hear the conclusion of the whole matter: fear God, and keep his commandments: for this is the whole duty of man. For God shall bring every work into judgment, with every secret thing, whether it be good or whether it be evil.**
>
> **Ecclesiastes 12:13-14**

Another truth, that the Lord has shown me, about obedience, is the need for a perfectly renewed mind. Enough emphasis cannot be put on a child of God, having the need for one. Basically because, according to the scriptures, without a renewed mind, we cannot obey what is God's good, acceptable, and perfect will. Without a renewed mind it will be utterly difficult, if not altogether impossible, to overcome the sinful and carnal tendencies, desires, and habits of the flesh. If you haven't been praying for one, now is a good time to start.

> I beseech you therefore, brethren, by the mercies of God, that ye present your bodies a living sacrifice, holy, acceptable unto God, which is your reasonable service, and be not conformed to this world: but be ye transformed by the renewing of your mind, that ye may prove what is that good, and acceptable, and perfect, will of God.
>
> Romans 12:12 <u>AMEN</u>

<u>FAITHFUL AND TRUE WITNESS</u>

> These things saith the amen, <u>the faithful and true witness.</u> The Beginning of the creation of God. I know thy works, that thou art neither cold nor hot: I would thou wert cold or hot. So then because thou art lukewarm, and neither cold nor hot, I will spue thee out of my mouth. Because thou sayest, I am rich, and increased with goods, and have need of nothing, and knowest not that thou art wretched, and miserable, and poor, and blind, and naked: I counsel thee to buy of me gold tried in the fire that thou mayest be rich; and white raiment, that thou mayest be clothed, and that the shame of thy nakedness do not appear and anoint thine eyes with eyesalve that thou mayest see. As many as I love, I rebuke, and chasten: Be zealous therefore, and repent. Behold, I stand at the door, and knock: If any man hear my voice, and open the door, I will come in to him, and will sup with him, and he with me.
>
> Revelation 3:14b-20

Jesus' statement about Himself, "the faithful and true witness," to me epitomizes the meaning of the exhortation to Laodicea, but also the whole "church" generational and worldwide (universal).

> But if we walk in the light, as He is in the light, we have fellowship one with another, and the blood of Jesus Christ His Son cleanseth us from all sin.
>
> John 1:7

When we give our heart to Christ, in place of spiritual poverty, we become spiritually rich, and as our walk with Christ developes, increased with spiritual goods.

Then said He unto them, therefore every scribe which is instructed unto the kingdom of heaven is like unto a man that is an householder, which bringeth forth out of his treasure things new and old.
Matthew 13:52

This scripture is in reference to the experiences we have as Christians, and the revelations God gives us as a result of those experiences, which give us knowledge and/or wisdom concerning the things of the kingdom of darkness, the kingdom of God, the kingdom of heaven, scripture, and/or for practical life application.

In Rev.3: 17, Jesus goes on to say, the Church says **"...and have need of nothing..."** Jesus then rebukes the Church for their self-deception; for as long as we live, we will never have need of nothing; for whether it be because of ourselves, the enemy, or other people, we will always be in need of something, especially from God.

The majority of true born-again Christians have a very limited understanding of what it is to be One with God, even to the point of self-deception, like the Laodicean church; which the revelation "...90% more or less," confirms. Therefore Jesus said, **...and knowest not that thou art wretched, and miserable, and poor, and blind, and naked...**

In reference to being partakers of the divine nature (2 Peter 1:4-10, 2 Timothy 3:16) God wrote through Peter, "...but he that lacketh these things is blind, and cannot see afar off, and hath forgotten that he was purged from his old sins." God doesn't want us to be wretched, miserable, poor, blind, and naked, having a form of godliness and powerless (denying the power thereof). His plea to His people is:

I counsel thee to buy of me gold tried in the fire that thou mayest be rich; and white raiment, that thou mayest be clothed, and that the shame of thy nakedness do not appear; and anoint thine eyes with eyesalve that thou mayest see.
Revelation 3:18

> Then shall the kingdom of heaven be likened unto ten virgins...five of them were wise and five were foolish...took no oil with them; but the wise took oil...behold the bridegroom cometh...the foolish said unto the wise, give us of your oil;... but the wise answered, not so;... but go ye rather to them that sell and buy for yourselves...
>
> **Matthew 25:1-13**

The Lord showed me that the five foolish are those who have a form of godliness (religion), who whether aware or unaware, realizing something is not right with their walk with Christ, try to pull the five wise down to their level of spiritual poverty, but the wise didn't <u>fall</u> for it. The "foolish virgins" do not know what it is to be <u>one</u> with God, to fellowship with Him, nor to be filled with the Holy Spirit. The "foolish virgins" do not know what it is to fight with demonic powers, and to be used by God concerning the gifts of the Holy Spirit.

<u>Without the Holy Spirit in our life we cannot become One with God, obey Him to the degree He desires of us, nor hear His voice telling us what to do and/or say from one moment to the next.</u> **Those who are led by the Spirit of God are the Sons of God,** Romans 8:14. Can we conclude then, that those who are not led by the Spirit of God are not His sons or daughters?

God used Peter to write, concerning the **divine nature:**

> **"..for if these things be in you, and abound, they make you that ye shall neither be barren nor unfruitful in the knowledge of our Lord Jesus Christ".**
>
> **(2 Peter 1:8)**

> **For the time is come that judgment must begin at the house of God and if it first begin at us, what shall the end be to them that obey not the Gospel of God?**
>
> **1 Peter 4:17**

Rev. 3:19;
> **As many as I love, I rebuke and chasten: be zealous therefore and repent.**

"But how will the world know unless all of us who make up the true body of Christ, repent of our slothfulness, slumber, deadness of Spirit and playing church, to be about doing Father's business (His desires and His alone), we must become One with God."

On September 22, 1997 the Lord gave me a song titled, **"Draw Near To The Wind,"** about revival.

Stanza Three:
> We must sing our praises unto him
> For the day of revival to begin
> This isn't all he wants us to do.
> Not only to love Him, but be <u>faithful and true.</u>

Chorus:
> Revival fire is blowing in the wind
> Calling God's people to draw closer to Him
> We must die to our will and our sin
> O ye people draw near to the wind

The wind is the Holy Spirit bringing revival fire to God's people.

Rev. 3:20
> **Behold I stand at the door, and knock, If any man hear my voice, and open the door, I will come in to him, and will sup with him and he with me.**

God wants to have a special relationship with us, that is wrapped in the kind of fellowship, that only being One with God can open up to us.

The door that Jesus is knocking on is the one that is found in the heart of those who profess to be His people saying, **"I want to have fellowship with you, the intimate kind, that is only found through being one with Me."** Therefore, He says to us, **"I counsel thee to buy of me."** Our dying to self-ambitions, self-desire, and self-will makes intimate fellowship with the Lord possible. **"I...will sup with him and he with me,"** is a fellowship with God, Jesus, and the Holy Spirit no words can adequately describe. It is fellowship that must be experienced to understand. Being One with God opens the door to the intimate fellowship God wants to have with us.

But he that is joined unto the Lord is one spirit.
1 Corinthians 6:17

Behold, I come as a thief. Blessed is he that watcheth, and keepeth his garments, lest he walk naked, and they see his shame.
Revelation 16:15

The nakedness spoken of in Revelation 3:17-18 and Revelation 16:15, is the lack of obedience (perfection in the flesh) observed by others, the lack of spirituality, the lack of maturity, and spiritual poverty that accompanies nominal-Christianity. **Our disobedience to the perfect will of God for our life leaves us naked, indecently exposed spiritually.** The nakedness is carnality, all of the wicked ambitions associated with the sinful nature that is manifested through the life of a disobedient and rebellious child. **Sin in our life causes us to be wretched, miserable, poor, blind, and naked.** The less death to self we entertain or engage in, the more evident these five facts are seen by others around us, and the worse a testimony for Jesus we are.

We are all different, although there are many similarities. Knowing how to overcome the sinful nature, disobedience in our life, self-will, self-desire, and self-ambition is different for each of us. Knowing how to overcome is dependent on what level we are affected, and our ability to comprehend or understand God's attempts to bring us into Oneness with Himself, to conform us into the exact image of Jesus.

Fasting is a device God has given us to overcome sin in our life; for some it needs to be done more often and more extreme than for others, it is only one device. We all must receive our own revelation of how to die to self. As I have written," it **is within the reach of everyone of us, if only we will seek the revealing of this truth from God, then receive it and run with it, (pursue it with all our life), (Mark 12:30)."**

Isaiah chapter 58 is misunderstood to be speaking of the blessings God bestows on those who fast food and/or drink. In Isaiah 58:5c God says: "Wilt thou call this a fast, and an acceptable day to the Lord?" God's reply in verse 6, "Is not this the fast that I have chosen? To loose the bands of wickedness..." With all that flows after this verse, the more excellent fast, in God's sight, is to forsake disobedience, the sinning lifestyle. **Jesus is our example of what being perfect in the sight of God is, He did nothing unless the Father told Him to, we are to do the same** (1 John 2:6, 1 Peter 21:22).

Isaiah 58:8-14 reveals what God will manifest through those of us who will obey God's perfect desire for our life. All this glory was manifested through Jesus, and can be manifested through us as well, if we will stop doing our desires, our will, and do GOD'S ONLY.

> **Then shall thy light break forth as the morning, and thine health shall spring forth speedily; and thy righteousness shall go before thee; the glory of the Lord shall be thy rereward. Then shalt thou call, and the Lord shall answer; thou shalt cry, and he shall say, here I am...then shall thy light rise in obscurity, and thy darkness shall be as the noon day; and the Lord shall guide thee continually, and satisfy thy soul in drought, and make fat thy bones; and thou shalt be like a watered garden, and like a spring of water, whose waters fail not. And they that shall be of thee shall build the old waste places: thou shalt raise up the foundations of many generations; and thou shalt be called the repairer of the breach, the restorer of the paths to dwell in...if thou...shall honor him, <u>not doing thine own ways, nor finding thine own pleasure, nor speaking thine own words: then shalt thou delight thyself in the Lord</u>; and I will cause thee to ride upon the high places of the earth...**
> **Isaiah 58:8-14**

All that God has given me to write about "Obedience, Being One With God," is to expose the Reader to this desire of God for us; and, in being exposed, he will begin to perform all of the truths written here in, in the Reader's life; and, in being performed, usher in a Worldwide Revival before the Church is taken out of the earth. The Worldwide Revival that is being prayed for, and has been prayed for, for decades.

CHAPTER 18
- THE MERCY OF GOD -

And that servant, which knew his lord's will, and prepared not himself, neither did according to his will, shall be beaten with many stripes. <u>But he that knew not, and did commit things worthy of stripes, shall be beaten with few stripes.</u> For unto whomsoever much is given, of him shall be much required: and to whom men have committed much, of him they will ask the more.

Luke 12:47-48

For as many as have sinned without law shall also perish without law: and as many as have sinned in the law shall be judged by the law; For not the hearers of the law are just before God, but the doers of the law shall be justified. <u>For when the Gentiles, which have not the law, do by nature the things contained in the law, these, having not the law, are a law unto themselves</u>: Which shew the work of the law written in their hearts, <u>their conscience also bearing witness</u>, and their thoughts the mean while accusing or else excusing one another; In the day when God shall judge the secrets of men by Jesus Christ according to my gospel.

Romans 2:12-16

As can be read in Luke 12:47-48, <u>the mercy of God only holds us accountable for revealed truth, not for what we do not know</u>. Those who know what He expects of us will be required of more than those who do not know the fullness of His expectation for us to be accepted and not rejected. **But when we are judged, we are chastened of the Lord, that we should not be condemned with the world (1 Corinthians 11:32).**

God will spend our lifetime to teach us to obey Him, because He does not want us to be condemned with the world, but if we choose not to comply with His correction (*rebel*), He will have no other option but to cast us away. With this written, I reiterate what I have written throughout this book, "God is the Judge." Paul said of himself, **But I keep under my body, and bring it into subjection: lest that by any means, when I have preached to others, I myself should be a castaway (1 Corinthians 9:27).**

Romans 2:12-16 is another example of God's mercy. If the Gospel has not been heard, God will judge a person after the law of their conscience. This takes care of the question concerning those who have not heard the Gospel.

The mercy of God is extended to the Struggler; the category for which the majority of us fit into who are "faithful and true." **My little children, these things write I unto you, that ye sin not. And if any man sin, we have an advocate with the Father, Jesus Christ the righteous: (1 John 2:1).** "If any man sin we have an advocate", is a consolation to those who are His faithful and true, who struggle to obey Him, whether or not they have the baptism of His power (the greater anointing of His Holy Spirit with whom the gifts are associated with) or not. This verse also serves to inform us that "IF" means that obedience is the norm for God's children, while disobedience is not.

It is those who are not the "faithful and true" (*Saints*), as we are required to be, who call themselves a Christian then live worldly and carnal lifestyles (*the Religious, Hypocrite, Lukewarm, and Backslider*) who will fall under the category of His wrath and judgment. **This book is written as an exhortation to obey Him and a warning of what could happen if we do not.** There is a balance for faith, grace, and works (*obedience*) for each one of us and only the Holy Spirit can help us to find it. The word of God is very adamant about the necessity for us to do good works to inherit eternal life (*those works the Holy Spirit tells us to do, obedience*).

Without obedience to the leadership of the Holy Spirit, we could be rejected by God, and be denied the salvation of our soul. For, those who are led by the Spirit of God are His children; not those who do what they think is right then expect God to pardon them. Jesus did not live a fully obedient life, suffer, die, and rise again to redeem us from the bondage of sin and death, to let us live rebellious anyway we want to lives. We are saved by grace through faith, and told to go onto perfection, which is obeying the Holy Spirit, moment by moment.

Jesus sacrificed all so that we could by faith in His redemptive work obey God (*go on to perfection*), and then at the end of our days, having been faithful and true, receive the salvation of our soul. The (*favor*) mercy of God is extended to those Believers who are like the Saints in the church of Philadelphia, and His judgment (*wrath*) is toward those Believers who are like the Believers in the church of Laodicea, lukewarm. There is an open door that no man can shut for the Saints who are like Philadelphia, but the Laodicean Believers have a closed door (the door of their heart) that only they can open and will not because they are lukewarm and do not desire to have an intimate relationship, and fellowship with God, being caught up in the affairs of this life rather than Him.

In 1982 a brother in the Lord and I were praying for the church service on a particular Sunday night, for God to do a number of things. All of which came to pass. I was in my second day of fasting and he in his first. As the service progressed, the Lord made real to me that there was a greater anointing above the congregation. The anointing was great in the service, but this anointing was awesome. I began to pray that he would pour if out on us, but He said, He could not because of the disobedience of the people. Two years later He told me what this greater anointing was; it was Holy Ghost Revival. Our disobedience hinders Revival, and the operation of the Holy Spirit not only in the church, but also in our life.

One final observation concerning these seven churches is how God began speaking to the churches with Ephesus, where He spoke of their lack of intimacy with Him, having lost their "first love." In His conversation with the last church, Laodicea, He finishes by bringing full circle this same theme, when knocking at the door of their heart, wanting intimacy with them, a time of fellowship," I will sup with him and he with me." God wants an intimate relationship with us; that is found in fellowshipping with Him. As He did with Adam so He wants to with us. It is this relationship with Him that will cause His anointing to flow through our lives as it did through Jesus that will bring in a great revival wherever we are.

CHAPTER 19
~ CONCLUSION ~

Although the Seven Churches of Asia, can be given a dispensational value, to describe seven different church ages, the spiritual condition of these seven churches has been evident in every generation. God has always had His faithful and true Saints, even in what is considered the "dark ages" of church history. There is a wellspring of historical information available that will attest to this fact. Also, I am not the only one who God has inspired to write about these seven churches as He has had me to write. Church history speaks of many Revivals over the centuries, we are overdue for one, and it is not God's fault it's ours.

The doctrine of SALVATION BY GRACE THROUGH FAITH has been so emphasized for centuries, with little attention devoted to good works, **works done in obedience to the dictates of the Holy Spirit, as He leads, guides, and directs us.** Many in the church see no purpose for true holiness, so they go about working out their own salvation according to the dictates of their own desires, instead of what God requires, His standard of holiness, His perfect will. For, so they say, God's grace and mercy will cover my disobedience (sin); to a certain degree this is true concerning God's "longsuffering", but in the end of our days, the lack of vigilance to change and **improve** in our obedience to His perfect will", could mean the loss of our eternal reward. As I have written throughout this book, "God is the judge of all such matters". Nonetheless, God's warning is clear, Rev. 2:5, 2:16, 3:13, 3:19...REPENT, and Rev. 3:5 "...and I will not blot out his name out of the book of life".

The lack of vigilance to get an informed knowledge of what God requires, and the lack of knowing that we are held accountable, by God, for the deeds we do in accordance to the dictates of the sinful nature bound in our flesh, cause many to fall far short of what God requires of us to be worthy of eternal life. It is this lack of diligence, and the willingness to compromise, that keeps a Believer bound in defeat, and of little value and use to God. God has given us the Power (*mighty power*) to overcome the temptations and desires of the sinful nature in our flesh.

God has given us the Power (*mighty power*) to obey His righteous nature planted in our spirit, to obey Him to the fullest of His dictates and expectations. His power (*mighty power*) makes us without excuse, so that in the day of judgment, like the friend spoken of in Matthew 22:12..."**and he was speechless**", so will we be. Only ten percent of professing "Christians" read their bible on a regular basis, thus knowing very little of what is expected of us by God to be saved at the end of our days. Many have gone into eternity believing they were worthy of salvation only to lose their own soul, for "many are called, but few are chosen."

But I keep under my body, and bring it into subjection: lest that by any means, when I have preached to others, I myself should be a castaway.

1 Corinthians 9:27

[*The same Greek word translated "castaway," in Hebrews 6:8 is translated "rejected." By definition these are the correct translation for the word - AAdmivn or Adokimos*]

For what is a man profited, if he shall gain the whole world, and lose his own soul? or what shall a man give in exchange for his soul?

Matthew 16:26

For many are called, but few are chosen.

Matthew 22:14

[*The context of this verse is in reference to those who choose not to comply with God's will and expectations (the Hypocrite, the Religious, and the Lukewarm); Matt. 22:1-13*]

Many English words have multiple meanings; an example is "works". Many Greek words are translated "works" in the Kings James version of the bible: humanitarian, physical labor, good deeds, our attitudes and behavior, etc. The most significant of these Greek words is obedience to a direct word from God spoken to us by His Holy Spirit to our spirit. We cannot obey God's voice, His directives, without the power the Holy Spirit gives us to obey God's perfect will, His standard of holiness that will cause us to be accepted instead of castaway and rejected.

All of us attend a church like one of these seven churches. In every church there are those who profess to be a Christian who live their life from one end of the spectrum of God's expectation to the other end. The Seven churches of Asia are the example of this fact. For those whose heart is not set on doing God's perfect will, if the church they are attending is not "worldly" enough and care free, they will just transfer their "letter" until they find one that is as "worldly" as they are. Is what I have written too straight, too narrow? A few would say, not for me, while the majority would say, yes. That is why the path to eternal life is narrow, and the one to eternal ruin is wide, not just for the unconverted Sinner, but also for all of those who refused to obey God, yet called themselves "Christian", for... **"Many are called but few are chosen."**

All scripture is given by inspiration of God, and is profitable for doctrine, for reproof, for correction, for instruction in righteousness:

2 Timothy 3:16

The Laity has a misconception that God requires less of them, concerning obedience and holy living, than He does the Minister, God requires the same "standard" for all of us. We are all called to be prophets (God's mouth piece), not only to the Church but also to the Lost. Some of us may never preach from a pulpit, but we are to preach (testify) to at least one, as God so leads us, (*"do the work of an evangelist"*)

To say that we are all God's children is not true. We are all God's creation, but not all of us are God's children. The attitude that as God's creation we are His children puts a Sinner on the same level as a Saint, thus falsely justifying rebellion (*disobedience*), and ultimately the Sinner never giving their "heart" to Christ. To say, I am a Sinner saved by grace is incorrect theology, for If I am saved by grace, I am no longer a Sinner.

For in God's sight, having been born-again, I am a Saint and no longer a Sinner. To say that I am a Sinner implies that I am still bound by the sinful nature, instead of set free from it, (*1 Peter 2:16, 1 John 3:9*).

We cannot live our life after the example of the world, the Hypocrite, the Religious, and the Lukewarm, in hope of eternal salvation. **To be accepted by God, we must live our life after the example of Jesus.** God is not satisfied with our "tip"; He wants all or nothing at all, (I would thou wert cold or hot...Rev. 3:15).

The need of the world today is crying out for the true children of God to live the example of Christ in their lives, to be tangible proof of the truth and reality that there is a God in heaven and in the world today. The world is wanting proof, that there is actually a Son of God, who lived, died for our sins, and rose from the grave with power and majesty, to signify to the world, that by virtue of His resurrection, He alone has been declared with power, that He is the Son of God and the only hope for the salvation of humanity, (Romans 1:4, 8:19). How will the world know, unless all of us who make up the true body of Christ, repent of our slothfulness, slumber, deadness of spirit, and playing church, to be about doing Father's business, (His desires and His alone)?

This is what I shared in the beginning paragraphs of this book: "The purpose of this book is not to be another exhortation to live holy, **but rather to obey God.** Holiness, piety, righteous living is the manifested fruit of obedience to God. The righteous nature of God that is planted in our spirit, when we repent of our sin, out of a heart of sincerity and truth (giving us the born-again experience), compels us to obey God. While it is the sinful nature that is still bound in our flesh that constantly wars against our performing what is our new nature to do, which is to obey God's perfect will for our life instead of sin."

It is true that we are saved by grace through faith and that there is nothing we can do, no good moral deed, nor anything that could merit salvation on our part. There is nothing that we can do that would cause God to pardon our sin and grant us access to eternal life, for the exception of repenting of our sin to accept God's gift of salvation, this God has established to be a fact. Good works do not save us, but holy living or more specifically, obedience to God's perfect will for our life, His every desire which He speaks to us being fulfilled, **after repentance,** guarantees the salvation of our soul through and by grace and faith when we pass from this life. **Once again hear God's warning to the Church, Rev. 2:5, 2:16, 3:13, 3:19 "...REPENT," and Rev. 3:5 "...<u>and I will not blot out his name out of the book of life</u>".**

When we walk in Jesus' example of obedience, we will be walking in "revival status." The gifts and fruits of the Holy Spirit will flow through our life unhindered and unrestricted as they did through Jesus' life. When we cease from doing our own works (*will*), then labor to enter into His rest (*His will*) [Hebrews 4:1-11], "Holy Ghost Revival" will hit the Church, then the World.

> **For the time is come that judgment must begin at the house of God: and if it first begin at us, what shall the end be of them that obey not the gospel of God?**
> **1 Peter 4:17**

− Sources −

1. *KJV of the Bible*
2. *Definition of NICOLAITANS, from Easton's Bible Dictionary, Robertson's Word Picture of the New Testament, Smith's Bible Dictionary*
3. *Meaning of the seven church names, from Hitchcock's Bible Names.*
4. *Greek word meanings, Strong Concordance.*
5. *Words from the song "Rise Up O Men of God" written by Wm. P. Merrill 1911.*
6. *Book cover, map of Asia Minor, from the website of "Jesus and Courageous Women of the Bible.*

~ About The Author ~

Samuel Robert Siders was born August 20, 1953 to Samuel Andrew Siders and Clara Ann Spencer-Siders in Columbus Ohio. Through a series of events, by age 15 the Lord made His love for him real in his life; making him aware that some day he would be saved, Samuel would even tell people who would try to win him to Jesus, that it is not time yet. For three and a half years the Holy Spirit did the work of bringing him to a radical life changing born again experience.

On July 8, 1972 while reading Matthew 14:30-31 about Peter walking on the sea to Jesus, then for fear of a storm Peter began to sink into the water. Peter cried out Lord save me. Matthew 14:31 states ... And immediately Jesus stretched forth His hand, and caught him, and said unto him, O thou of little faith, wherefore didst thou doubt? The Holy Spirit touched Samuel's heart with how much Jesus loved Peter when Jesus "immediately" stretched out His hand to catch him. At that moment of revelation, the Holy Spirit told Samuel, Now it is time. Samuel gave his heart to Christ and has served Him to this day.

Here is Samuel's account; "Now it is time" was a special calling for me to repent, because of the Calling God has placed on my life, for this point in time that He has given me to live. I have yet to fully understand or fathom what "Now it is time" means, but He has assured me that I will have fulfilled my Calling before I die."

While in a church service, July 2004 the Lord called him to preach. As a result of this call of God on his life he enrolled in the Appalachian District School Of Ministry (ADSOM) in Ghent, West Virginia.

God requires far more of us than most Believers are willing to live. Refusing to comply could mean being rejected at the Judgement. This book contains a message all Believers need to hear.

E-mail address to correspond with the author: samuside@aol.com

Domain name for direct access to order more books:
www.thesevenchurchesofasia.com

To order books by phone, call toll free: 1-888-280-7715

AuthorHouse web address to self-publish your book:
www.authorhouse.com

CPSIA information can be obtained at www.ICGtesting.com
Printed in the USA
LVOW131104220412

278633LV00003B/131/A